Enough

Heal Your Relationship

with Food and Body

Using Attachment Theory

Tiffany North, RN, BSN

RECALIBRATED
NORTH PRESS

"Tiffany North's work on attachment theory in *Enough* offers one of the most intersectional approaches in the field, taking into account the effects of diet culture trauma, race, queerness, fatness, and disability. She actually acknowledges ways that systemic oppression shapes relational patterns, survival strategies, and our capacity to feel safe with others. Her compassionate, justice-rooted framework invites us to reimagine attachment as a reflection of collective and generational resilience. She does this in a manner that is both accessible and captivating."

—ANGEL AUSTIN (she/her) is a Fat Liberationist,
an Anti-Racism Activist, a Disability Justice Advocate,
and the Creator of Sacred Space for Fat Bodies

"This book doesn't hand you another set of food rules—it hands you the truth. With fierce clarity and a trauma-informed lens, Tiffany guides us to an understanding of how attachment wounds fuel our struggles with food and body image. The author—who I know and respect—brings her brilliance, boldness, and a no-bullshit approach to healing. If you're ready to stop trying harder and start feeling whole, this book is for you. It's honest, it's liberating—and it just might change everything."

—DAWN NICKEL, PHD,
Founder, SHE RECOVERS® Foundation

"*Enough* is one of the most compelling and insightful books on Intuitive Eating to be published in recent years. Nurse Tiffany brings a fresh, deeply compassionate voice to this space, skillfully weaving personal stories and helpful analogies. What sets this book apart is her powerful integration of attachment theory and how it shapes our relationship with food. *Enough* offers a meaningful, accessible path for anyone looking to dig deeper into healing their relationship with food and body. It's not just informative—it's transformative."

—Sumner Brooks, MPH, RDN,
co-author of *How to Raise an Intuitive Eater*

Library of Congress Control Number: 2025911377

ISBN (paperback): 979-8-9991046-7-0
ISBN (ebook): 979-8-9991046-8-7
ISBN (audiobook): 979-8-9991046-9-4

Book design and production by Domini Dragoone, Sage Folio Creative
Cover images: cherry © Lisa from Pexels/Pexels, leaf © Ultima/123rf, gingham © Desifoto/iStock
Author photo © Credit to whichever one of you glorious humans took this, you know who you are.

Published by Recalibrated North Press
Portland, Oregon
www.coachtiffanyrn.com

 @coachtiffanyrn

*For anyone who doesn't yet
know it in your bones,
you're good enough,
just as you are.*

Contents

I believe

in you.

Author's Note

You aren't here to simply heal. You're here to live, to experience life in all its richness. I'm inspired by the song "Healing is Not My Purpose" by Toni Jones. The song reminds us that purpose is more than personal growth; purpose is found in living, experiencing joy, feeling pleasure, and prioritizing soul satisfaction.

When expressing appreciation for our bodies during a group coaching session, a client said, "my body houses my soul." Her words brought the song to mind, and a lightbulb went off in my brain.

You can satisfy your soul by listening to your body.

When I shared this concept, another dear client responded in a quivering voice, "And my body doesn't even ask for that much." It pierced my heart to hear that. Why do we deny our bodies and our souls what they ask for?

Your body, your soul, has been clamoring for attention, acceptance, nurturance, trust, pleasure, joy, and satisfaction. It's time to satisfy your soul, which means satisfying your body. Healing is a means to this end.

What will it take to satisfy your soul? Let's find out and do exactly that.

Ready to explore? You might want a dedicated journal for this experience. Reading with a group of like-minded friends might also be helpful. Do whatever works best for your learning style. Create space for this work; change takes time and intention.

Terms

There are some terms I use in a different way than you may be used to, and some terms you may not know at all. This isn't an exhaustive list, just the few that I felt needed to be clarified right up front. Some are definitions I've personally formed from my reading and training, which I'm sharing so you know how I intend for them to be read. Some are definitions from websites or other experts but are in line with my usage of them. Additionally, some terms need to be examined from a different lens than the common uses in our culture.

Attachment Theory: Attachment theory was pioneered by psychiatrist and psychoanalyst John Bowlby, who was basically raised by a nanny. He realized that your formative relationship with your caregivers matters deeply in how you move through and experience the world and how you show up in relationships. Subsequent researchers, including psychologist Mary Ainsworth, developed this concept further, creating the attachment styles (MindOnly, 2025). Today, attachment theory is often used in therapy and self-help for adults struggling in relationships. If you want to read more on the subject, you can find additional resources at the end of the book.

Binge: This term is fraught with stigma. Bingeing generally isn't well defined, and most people use the term very casually. Some people think eating two cookies, eating beyond fullness, or having seconds is bingeing (it's not). There are criteria and screening tools for binge-eating disorder, but they don't account for the impact of restriction (which often causes primal hunger). The screenings most often use subjective questions, which of course would be skewed for someone who has dieted a lot or has an eating disorder. I use this term when referring to the way someone describes their own eating patterns or to describe a type of eating that feels out of control. Eating in a way that feels out of control isn't proof of anything but likely means there's an unmet need. There's an entire chapter on bingeing later.

Body Mass Index (BMI): The (bogus) BMI is antiquated and was never meant to be a measure of individual health. Additionally, the (bogus) BMI was made for white men and insurance tables. The categories were arbitrarily changed and influenced by weight loss drug companies.

The (bogus) BMI causes fat people to be stigmatized and to receive poor medical treatment and for real health concerns to be overlooked in both fat and thin people. Check out the resources at the end of the book if you'd like to learn more.

Diets: I define diets/dieting and restriction/restricting as cutting out any food or food group because they're "bad" or you "shouldn't" eat them, reducing the amount of food you eat or the time frame in which you eat, attempting to ignore or suppress hunger, or any other attempt to manipulate what or when you eat for the purpose of trying to be thinner or manipulate the aesthetic of your body (even if you're trying to lose weight to be "healthy" or calling it a lifestyle). However, using discernment when eating is NOT dieting. More on this later.

Disordered eating: Disordered eating has generally been used to describe concerning patterns of eating that don't fit within the diagnostic criteria for an eating disorder. Many people that come to work with me feel relief when they hear this term because it helps them feel seen in their struggles.

While I've used this term to describe myself and clients, and I use it a few times in this book, I don't love this term. Unfortunately, due to diet culture, people often believe that their normal need to eat enough is disordered eating. Additionally, I think the term further perpetuates the idea that there's something wrong with you if you have challenges in your relationship with food. Using the word "disordered" to describe relationships with food adds to the shame in an already painful situation. It also implies that the way you've survived was wrong. "Disordered" eating is adaptive; it's a way you've kept yourself safe, regulated, and alive. Your eating patterns may not fully align with how you'd like to relate to food (and we'll work on that!) but it isn't something to shame yourself over either.

Eating disorders: An eating disorder is a clinical diagnosis as defined by *The Diagnostic and Statistical Manual of Mental Disorders, Fifth Edition* (DSM-5). Most frequently talked about and diagnosed are anorexia, bulimia, and binge-eating disorder.

Anorexia in people who aren't thin is called atypical anorexia, creating a misperception that fat people don't experience malnutrition from anorexia. This creates harm. For example, medical providers don't give suitable care or appropriately screen people in larger bodies for eating disorders. Fat people are often applauded for food restriction, even when it's dangerous and extreme. Being encouraged by your doctor to develop or continue eating disorder patterns can be catastrophic.

Diet culture in healthcare perpetuates the harmful misconception that fat people must have binge-eating disorder. Fat people can have any type of eating disorder, or none at all. People of any size can develop any type of eating disorder. Additionally, many of the screening tools used to determine if someone has an eating disorder are biased and don't filter for diet culture, food restriction, or anti-fatness.

Lastly, eating disorder treatment isn't accessible to all who suffer, and it most often isn't culturally competent, so BIPOC, LGBTQIA2s+ people, and disabled folks don't have access to the services they need and are frequently harmed by the available treatment options, creating medical trauma.

Fat: I use the terms fat and larger body interchangeably, and language is important. Our resistance to the word fat is rooted in cultural bias because the idea that fat is bad is so deeply ingrained. Fat is not bad. For me and many people, using the word fat is tied to fat liberation and accepting our bodies as they are. It's also a message to the world that we're humans who deserve to be treated with the same respect as thin people.

Some people prefer the term fat, some don't. While fat is a descriptor, and should be neutral like tall, our culture has attached stigmas to it. The phrase, "people in larger bodies" is often used as a more neutral descriptor. Still not ideal, but it's less stigmatized. I'll use both terms in this book, larger for those who prefer it and fat to reclaim the term fat as neutral and normalize its use.

If you're thin, calling other people fat isn't a great idea unless you know they're comfortable claiming the term for themselves, such as when referring to a fat activist. Ask yourself why you're referring to their body size in the first place. If it's to be helpful, such as when planning an outing with a group of friends and wanting to ensure the seating is adequate, consider asking, "Does the seating accommodate larger bodies?" rather than singling out one person. If their size is truly pertinent information and you don't know the person's preferred term, you might use larger body instead of fat. Please don't use overweight, ob*se, and especially never morbidly ob*se in referring to someone else's body (more on these terms to come).

Fategories: From Linda Gerhardt of the *Fluffy Kitten Party* blog, the fat spectrum, aka fategories, speaks to the differences in lived experience based on size or fatness. For example, someone who is small fat (U.S. women's size 18 or 1-2x or below), can't always find clothes that fit, but there are retailers that have their sizes. They can find seating that works in most public spaces. They may experience medical trauma based on weight stigma and anti-fat bias, especially if they're disabled or have chronic illnesses. But someone who is infinifat (U.S. women's size 34 or 6x and above) will have a very different experience with much more marginalization. They usually won't be able to find clothes that fit at brick-and-mortar stores and size out of the vast majority of retailers, even online. They'll most often not find accessible seating or appropriate medical equipment. They'll experience more bias in medical settings, and a tremendous amount of harmful treatment as they go about their lives.

In other words, as size increases, marginalization increases in very significant and impactful ways. (Gerhardt, 2025)

The fategories: The fat categories and names aren't universally agreed upon. People have the right to identify however they'd like. And it's important to recognize that there's meaningful history around how the terms evolved. There are also limitations to these terms. For example, sizes are based on US women's sizes, which isn't ideal as other genders aren't represented, but using these sizes is still helpful so we can understand how some experiences are similar and some very different.

- straight size: not fat, can find chairs and clothes that fit everywhere
- small fat: below 18, or 1x – 2x
- mid fat: 20 – 24 or 26, or 2x – 3x
- large fat: 26 to 32, or 4x – 5x
- superfat: 26 and up
- infinifat: 32 – 34 and above (may be used as a variant of superfat)

Health at Every Size®: Health at Every Size® (HAES®) is a concept and set of principles developed by the Association of Size Diversity and Health (ASDAH). HAES® shifts healthcare away from weight-centric care to empowering people of all sizes in accessing respectful and responsive health care. As a HAES®-aligned provider, this means that I care for and offer support to clients in the body they're in now, without assuming it needs to be changed. In other words, I don't add to stigma against fat people or gatekeep care by telling people they need to lose weight. Agency, bodily autonomy, consent, and social justice are foundational to my practice.

We all deserve care and support in the pursuit of health, in the way that feels aligned for us personally, free from harmful bias. I highly recommend reading the principles and history in full on their website ASDAH.org.

Marginalized identities: People who are marginalized (think *pushed to the edges*) by our cultural norms and systems of oppression and inequality due to an identity they hold. It isn't that having an identity is causing their marginalization; it's our culture causing marginalization.

This prejudice almost always impacts people with non-white ethnicities. The types of harm and inequities are unique among people who are Black, Indigenous, Latinx, Pacific Islander, Asian, Middle Eastern, or multiracial, for example, but are all significant. Some of these groups experience more systemic oppression and blatant racism than others due to structural inequities. This is described well in Isabel Wilkerson's book *Caste*.

There are also identities unrelated to race or ethnicity that are marginalized, such as disabled people, LGBTQIA2s+ people (especially transgender people), fat people, neurodivergent people, people who struggle with addiction, people living in poverty, houseless people, and more. The more intersecting marginalized identities one holds, the more inequity and othering increases. For example, a low-income, visibly disabled, infinifat, trans, black woman will experience more harm from these systems than a small-fat white woman with non-visible disabilities (like me).

Ob*se: I use an asterisk as this word is a slur. It's harmful. It's a category of the (bogus) BMI and using it causes increased stigma and harm. The Latin root of this word means "to have eaten oneself fat." There are many reasons a person might be fat, most often genetic, medical, and environmental. Morbidly ob*se implies someone will die due to their size. No one's death can be predicted, and categorizing someone as "morbid" is wrong. Everyone deserves respect and appropriate medical care, regardless of size.

Orthorexia: an obsession with eating "healthy" or perfectly, to the point of restriction and fear of many foods (National Eating Disorders Association, 2025).

Overweight: Over what weight? But seriously, this is from the (bogus) BMI and implies there's a right weight to be. Weight has so many determining factors. And it changes over a lifetime, as it should.

Thin privilege: Privileges that a person holds simply because they're thin, such as being more likely to get a job, or doctors providing treatment for their symptoms rather than telling them to just lose weight. Thin privilege also provides more access to basic needs like comfortable seating, clothing that fits at most stores, and properly sized medical equipment.

Whiteness: I refer to being white to illustrate that, due to white supremacy in our current culture, I've been granted privilege simply because of the color of my skin. For example, if the police are called, I'm likely to be believed and very unlikely to be harmed by the police.

However, using the terms "white" or "whiteness" is a commonly used way of naming the racist and classist systems that create oppression and inequality. It may also be used to call out an individual's behavior when their behavior is upholding those systems.

White supremacy: The idea that whiteness is the standard, better than, and deserving of more recognition. It's an umbrella term encompassing the systems that support the false bias that some people (white people) deserve privileges over others.

From the Racial Equity Tools Glossary:

The idea (ideology) that white people and the ideas, thoughts, beliefs, and actions of white people are superior to People of Color and their ideas, thoughts, beliefs, and actions. While most people associate white supremacy with extremist groups like the Ku Klux Klan and the neo-Nazis, white supremacy is ever present in our institutional and cultural assumptions that assign value, morality, goodness, and humanity to the white group while casting people and communities of color as worthless (worth less), immoral, bad, and inhuman and "undeserving." Drawing from critical race theory, the term "white supremacy" also refers to a political or socio-economic system where white people enjoy structural advantage and rights that other racial and ethnic groups do not, both at a collective and an individual level (Equity in the Center, 2025).

The Whims of Diet Culture

My food and body story is heavy. It's exhausting. It's old. I didn't put my story here because this book is about YOU and how to finally heal your relationship with food and your body. Buuuut, I know some people want to read my WHOLE STORY. Don't worry, it's in Appendix A.

I'm sure if you're reading this book, your story feels the same. You already know this story. It's yours, your mother's, your grandmother's, and your friends' stories. It may have been your father's story. If you have a child, you might be desperately hoping it won't become their reality too.

> *It's the story of our ongoing, generational struggle with diets (restriction) and food.*

The grandmother stories wreck me. They're the hardest because I think about all those decades of suffering. Recently, a client told me her grandmother didn't want to shop for a dress to wear to my client's wedding because she needed to "lose five pounds first." Her grandmother was 80 years old. She never found relief.

Being at the whims of diet culture (the systems in place that value thinness and appearance over all else) and caught in a constant battle with your body is exhausting and disempowering.

These stories have been passed down, inherited, over and over and over. I know we share similar experiences. I hear these stories echoed endlessly. You've probably felt like you needed to lose weight or at least felt shitty about your body or your eating habits. You've probably told yourself thousands of times that you NEED to get your shit together, eat "healthy," and exercise more. You've probably believed you'd finally be happy if you did get said shit together. But that belief only made you feel worse.

Maybe you started dieting (restricting) before puberty or sometime in your teens. Maybe you felt like managing food was too hard or someone tried to control your food experiences, so you didn't bother with dieting (restricting) and went the route of the rebel. Maybe you just ate whatever but still felt bad about it. Maybe you oscillated between eating nothing and eating everything. No matter what you did to survive it, you felt like a crappy failure, and magazines, social media, TV, your family and friends, and even your doctor reinforced it all.

Growing up in the US, I heard soooo many of those messages. Over and over, I was exposed to the messages that there was something wrong with my body. And, of course, I listened. I raged against my body. I hated it. I tried to contort my body to fit their standards. I tried so hard to control and manage it. It never worked—at least, not for long. And it certainly never made me feel good in the long term. It took years of learning and healing, but now I know it's the message that there's something wrong with me that I need to fight against, *not my body*.

My body is
my ally,
my home,
not my enemy.

Somewhere along the line, over and over and over, you got the message that there's something wrong with you, and the only way to be good enough is to change, to "fix" yourself by controlling and managing food and your body. If you tried to change, chances are that you couldn't, at least not in the long term, so then you got the message that you weren't doing it right and you needed to do it better—to do it HARDER.

> *How's that working for you? Yeah. Me neither.*
> *How long have you been doing this? Decades?*
>
> *That's Enough.*

We're not going to try HARDER anymore. Screw feeling shitty or like a failure. We're done with that.

Instead, like a phoenix, it's time to rise from the smoldering ashes… out of the decades of misery in the dumpster fire of diet culture BS and into a peaceful relationship with food and your body.

Will this book teach you how to lose weight? Nope. Doesn't work. Fuck that.

Will it teach you to try harder to control food? Nope. Fuck that too.

Will it give you the ideal meal plan to finally find peace? Nope. There's no such thing.

And even if there was, trying to follow it would only make you feel like a failure. Again, we're done with that.

It WILL start you on a journey to heal your relationship with your*self*, with food, and your body. It'll empower you to *know deeply* that you aren't broken. It'll show you how to trust yourself. It'll point you in the direction of finally satisfying your soul.

This book will teach you to deeply nurture yourself; how to be at home in and make peace with your body, exactly as it is, not how you or anyone else thinks it "should" be.

My body is the only thing with me
through my entire life, carrying me
through life's experiences, bringing
me to who I am in this moment.

My body is my home,
refuge from life's sharp edges, my own
private island in a stormy sea.

My body is my compass,
showing me what I need and guiding
the way to where I want to be.

My body is my vessel, allowing me
to feel everything. Pleasure and pain,
anger and fear, sadness and joy.

My body is my beloved quilt, holding
me and keeping me warm.

I love all its colors, seams, and frayed edges.

My body is my dear friend.
It always was.
Today, I reciprocate.

I want this for you too.

No matter where you are in your relationship with food and your body, you're in the right place. If you struggle with food or body image, if you would like it to be different, if you feel shame about it, you're in the right place. No matter how your challenges show up—hating your body, hyperfixating on or ignoring your body, hating food or loving food, eating everything or eating nothing, or eating nothing and then everything—you're in the right place.

> *There are no prerequisites.*

In this book, you'll find solace, understanding, clarity, and a path to peace with food and your body. But more than that, you'll find a way to feel secure in yourself, to finally be at home in your body. Most importantly, you'll find empowerment.

I can help you because I've lived the decades of misery. Because I rose from the ashes. Because I know your story intimately. And yes, I have knowledge, training, credentials,[1] and the experience supporting people to finally heal.

But most importantly, I can help you because I believe in you. I know this isn't your fault. I know you can heal, given the right tools and support.

> *I believe in you.*

---

1. RN, BSN, Integrative Nurse Coach, Certified Intuitive Eating Professional, SHE RECOVERS® coach, Embodied Eating Disorder Recovery training, and the list goes on…

Chapter One

The Lie of Diet Culture

"Diet culture is a system of beliefs and practices that elevates thin bodies above all others, often interpreting thinness as a sign of both health and virtue. It mandates weight loss as a way of increasing social status, strengthening character, and accessing thin privilege."

—Aubrey Gordon, *What We Don't Talk About When We Talk About Fat*

A ubrey Gordon, also known as Your Fat Friend, is an author, podcaster, and activist. She writes about fatness, fat acceptance, and anti-fat bias, and her podcast, *Maintenance Phase*, focuses on the poor science behind many health and wellness fads.

I chose to put Aubrey Gordon's definition here first intentionally. Thin people's voices dominate in intuitive eating, anti-diet, and eating disorder treatment spaces, and Gordon offers a definition from the perspective of someone who has experience navigating oppression in our anti-fat society, weight bias, and diet culture.

In the intro of the book *You Are Your Best Thing* by Tarana Burke and Brené Brown, Brown says that experience trumps academia. I fully believe that, especially in matters where there are such heavy biases like weight stigma.

With weight stigma and anti-fat bias so heavily infused in our health care system and research, we must look at the lived experiences of folks in fat bodies over the (biased) research. I've read every one of Brené Brown's books. While they helped me learn and grow, I'm acutely aware of her past use of anti-fat language and promotion of diets. It's so hard to navigate one's own well-being and constantly have to weed out the harmful messages from the helpful. In the Resources section, check out the open letter to Brené Brown by Anna Chapman that speaks to this painful nuance poignantly.

As much as I've tried to create a safe space to land in this book, free from stigma, shame, or harm, I know that it isn't possible because our cultural understanding is always evolving (and so is mine). I commit to listening and learning. I want to acknowledge my thin privilege and white privilege and know that while I'm the creator of the food and body attachment model and the expert in this book, I don't have the same lived experiences as someone who has experienced serious oppression due to weight stigma (I've experienced it only in small doses). I'm considered ob*se by (bogus) BMI standards, but I'm small fat, and the holder of a few marginalized identities that are mostly not visible.[2] I'm therefore not an expert when it comes to body acceptance for people with mid-fat bodies and up, especially when they have multiple visible marginalized identities in the systems of inequality that make it so hard to navigate through our culture.

As Sabrina Strings illustrates in *Fearing the Black Body: The Racial Origins of Fat Phobia*, weight stigma and anti-fat bias are deeply rooted in white supremacy, and the impact is much worse for people who hold more than one marginalized identity, especially when easily visible. It's my intention to include voices of people who are better suited to speak to that experience.

---

2. Be sure to read the terms at the beginning of the book, it's captivating, lol. But seriously, it's helpful info.

We are not
our size.

Hearing the voices of people who have been harmed by systems of oppression and inequality brings a sharper focus and deeper understanding of the impact these experiences have. Understanding is a critical part of change.

Seeing yourself in the media you consume is powerful and healing. Unfortunately, representation is a privilege not everyone has access to. Due to the level of dehumanization of fat people built into our cultural messaging, it's important that we see ourselves represented authentically. Additionally, seeing fat people simply living reminds us all that fat people are real people with full and complex lives.

I encourage you to look at your bookshelf and media feed. What do you see? A bunch of content produced by thin, white, able-bodied men and women? Be intentional and consume media by folks with a variety of lived experiences and marginalized identities, especially those with fat bodies. One of the books I personally love and recommend is *The Body is Not an Apology* by Sonya Renee Taylor. So worth the read. You can find a list of recommended books at the end of this book.

The Lie of Diet Culture

Diet culture messaging shames us into thinking there's something wrong with us. The "solutions" the diet industry and diet culture offer keep you stuck in the cycle of dieting/restriction and self-loathing. These "solutions" are largely provided by people trying to make big bucks. Diets (restricting) make challenges with food and body worse. Diet culture only serves to make you feel like you aren't good enough (so that you'll buy, stay quiet, be easier to control, etc.).

Special message to those who haven't experienced the restrict/binge cycle: this section may feel like it doesn't apply to you. Reading through it will still help.

First off, even if you don't restrict, you may still have restrictive thinking or "shoulds" about food. This mentality impacts your relationship with food, even if you end up eating all the things you think you "shouldn't."

Challenges with food and body relationships can show up in all sorts of ways. It can show up as the restrict/binge/shame cycle, food and body avoidance, hating your body, or eating like a 12-year-old—aka being in fuck-it mode for your whole life. All of these patterns have two things in common: dissatisfaction and shame.

Many of these patterns are rooted in the same internalized diet culture messages. You'll likely relate to and see yourself in the patterns, even the behaviors that you don't fully identify with. When we get to the food and body attachment styles in Chapter 4, you'll notice that you probably have some characteristics from each of the types or have experienced different types at various points in your life. No one fits perfectly into one box.

If you're struggling with food or body image, it's not your fault. You aren't defective. Diet culture is selling you the lie that there's something wrong with you if you don't look a certain way or eat "perfectly." Growing up under the influence of diet culture adds shame—and shame makes *everything worse.*

IT'S NOT YOUR FAULT.

Your relationship with food and your body is largely the result of your life experiences, modeling by caregivers, messages you received from harmful systems, and your biology/wiring. It isn't the result of any personal shortcomings or because there's something inherently wrong with you.[3]

First, let's dig into the impact of the harmful cultural messages that influence your relationship with food and your body. We're all

---

3. In fact, I'd argue there's something inherently RIGHT with you.

mired in it, swimming in the same toxic environment and breathing it in daily. It can be so difficult to see clearly. These messages are deeply ingrained and pervasive, which makes it extremely difficult to separate the internalized cultural messages from our own beliefs.

> "When I put down what is not mine to carry, I am free. Free to call in peace with each breath. Free to be at home wherever I am. Free to walk a path of profound liberation with each step I take."
> —Octavia F. Raheem, *Gather*

What is Diet Culture – Definition

I like the nuance and comprehensiveness of Registered Dietitian Christy Harrison's[4] definition of diet culture:

Diet culture is a system of beliefs that:

- Worships thinness and equates it to health and moral virtue, which means you can spend your whole life thinking you're irreparably broken just because you don't look like the impossibly thin "ideal."
- Promotes weight loss as a means of attaining higher status, which means you feel compelled to spend a massive amount of time, energy, and money trying to shrink your body, even though the research is very clear that almost *no one* can sustain intentional weight loss for more than a few years.
- Demonizes certain ways of eating while elevating others, which means you're forced to be hyper-vigilant about your eating, ashamed of making certain food choices, and distracted from your pleasure, your purpose, and your power.

---

4. Christy is a thin white woman. And I felt this was still helpful to include. I really appreciate the way her definition speaks to the disproportionate harm of the systems of oppression.

- Oppresses people who don't match up with its supposed picture of "health," which disproportionately harms women, femmes, trans folks, people in larger bodies, people of color [especially Black and Indigenous people], and people with disabilities, damaging both their mental and physical health [because is it based on the thin, white "ideal"]. (Harrison, 2025)

For decades, I was stuck in the restrict/binge/hate myself cycle (from about age 10 to my mid-thirties). I didn't know there was another way. I bought the lies of diet culture. I thought I had to be thin to be a good nurse and coach. I thought that self-love meant I would be thin, fit, eating perfectly, working out 5+ days a week, and so evolved I'd be practically levitating.

We get these messages from all over the place, but for me, some of the most damaging were directly from women I looked up to. Everywhere I looked, I saw women leaders promoting dieting (restriction). If you're a boomer or GenXer, you had a front row seat to Oprah's endless diets (everything from the liquid diet to WeightWatchers). Oprah's pursuit of thinness connected her to millions of people who struggled with body image. We were mesmerized.

While researching for this book, I did a quick google search of "Oprah's diet" and tons of articles on what Oprah eats in a day came up (written recently, even). It's so tragic to me; she has so much more to offer than a list of foods she eats. Did you know you can even read all about Oprah's day-to-day diet on her website, like, EXACTLY what she supposedly ate? No wonder we're all preoccupied with food and our bodies.

But she's only one of many… from Brené Brown and keto/paleo to Gwyneth Paltrow and intuitive fasting,[5] our women leaders are

---

5. Intuitive fasting is a DIET and an attempt to confuse people who want to be intuitive eaters. Fasting = restriction, and restriction = a DIET.

promoting the pursuit of thinness.[6] Some of these leaders say they're body-positive, telling us that we're beautiful even if we're bigger… but this talk is shallow. They say their goal is to be "healthy." After losing weight, they talk about how great they feel. How they *finally* feel good about their body. Their resulting message is thinness = BETTER. In other words, once you wear a certain size or weigh less, then you can finally accept yourself and be happy, desired, and successful.

In addition to the women leaders I followed, this message came at me from almost every angle: my personal doctors, the doctors and healthcare workers I worked alongside, social media, family, friends, fitness spaces… the list goes on and on.

Sadly, it's true: in our culture, thin people have higher status, aka thin privilege, and people in less accepted (fat) bodies are oppressed.

Yeah, but… isn't thin better?

Better than what? Fat? Aside from thin privilege, it isn't. Having a thin body[7] doesn't mean you live any longer, especially when controlled for health-promoting behaviors like eating veggies, having close relationships, or not smoking.

Even if you have a thin body, you can still hate yourself. Having a thin body doesn't make you morally superior. The idea that thin is more attractive is weight stigma, desirability politics, and internalized anti-fat bias, born in racist roots. If you want to learn more, I highly recommend the books *Fearing the Black Body* by Sabrina Strings and *Belly of the Beast* by Da'Shaun L. Harrison.

---

6. There's a reason diet companies get superstars to endorse their products. I'll give you 3 guesses… 1) $ 2) $ and 3) $$$$$$$$$$$$$$$$$$$$$$$$$$$$ to the tune of billions (at your expense).

7. Do you HAVE a body? Are you IN a body? Are you A body? Yes, I did, in fact contemplate deep existential questions such as these and had many robust convos about them when writing this book. Anyway, I think we have a body, are in a body, and are our body at the same time. But you can read it in the way that makes sense to you. :)

If you're still unsure if thin is better than fat, let's look at your beliefs. Try this exercise I adapted from Marilyn Wann and Tracy Brown, RD. Spend a few minutes free writing on each of the following:

First, fill in the blank with as many things you associate with fatness as you can think of.
Fat =

Next, do the same with thinness.
Thin =

Then, answer the following questions:
- Where and when did you learn these associations?
- What behaviors are you prone to that attempt to seek thinness or avoid fatness?
- What is your body's experience of these attempts?
- What behaviors reflect an avoidance of shame around your body and eating?
- How do your attempts to avoid shame backfire?

Give yourself some compassion and self-care time. These things are painful to look at. If you want an expanded version of this exercise, check out Marilyn Wann's video in the Resources section.

Remember, this wiring didn't come from you. In the words of Shilo George, body sovereignty activist and racial justice consultant, about internalized anti-fat bias: "This wiring is like an invasive species. It isn't yours or from you, but now that it's taken root, it's all tangled up in your business. And it will take effort to root it out."

We all take on this shame as a result of internalized diet culture messaging. We see that the world treats thin people better, and we want access to that privilege, that love and approval, so we blame our bodies and strive to be thin. The actual shame is that our culture tells us we have to look or be a certain way to be worthy of love and approval. This shame belongs to a culture that asks us to reject ourselves to fit in. Diet culture harms all of us.

In this book, we'll look at those internalized messages, root them out, and dismantle them. It's time to replace those messages with the knowledge that your value and worth are inherent. You are enough, just as you are. You've been enough through all of it and will continue to be.

Have you had enough?
Enough shame.

Ingested enough?
Enough diet culture BS.

Hated yourself enough?
Enough fighting your body.

Exercised enough?
Enough chasing thinness.

Beat yourself up enough?
Enough trying HARDER.

Have you had enough?
Enough feeling like you're never good enough.

When I finally healed my relationship with food and my body, it really meant healing my relationship with my whole self. In large part, it was understanding my value and worth didn't change if my body did. My value is constant and inherent. When people asked me what that was like… the only way I could describe healing was going from thinking in my head that my value was constant and inherent to knowing, feeling, and believing it in my *bones*.

You're already enough. Turns out, you always were. And, in theory, you know this. It's time to learn it in your bones. Time to build a solid foundation. Let's get to it.

Chapter Two

Intuitive Eating: An Alternative to Dieting

ietitians Evelyn Tribole and Elyse Resch recognized the problems with diets (restriction) in the early nineties. They saw the
writing on the wall. Clients would come to them and receive dietary
recommendations. The diets may have "worked" temporarily, but
inevitably, their clients wouldn't be able to maintain it. Worse than
the diets simply not working, the clients would have more shame
after each failed attempt. From that observation, in a desire to truly
support clients, they developed the Intuitive Eating framework.

From the Intuitive Eating website:

"Intuitive Eating is a practice, which honors both physical and
mental health. Intuitive Eating is aligned with Health at Every Size®,
because the pursuit of intentional weight loss is a failed paradigm,
which creates health problems: including weight stigma, weight
cycling, and eating disorders. All bodies deserve dignity and respect."

—Evelyn Tribole, 2025

The Ten Principles of Intuitive Eating:

1. Reject Diet Culture
2. Honor Your Hunger
3. Make Peace with Food
4. Discover the Satisfaction Factor
5. Feel Your Fullness
6. Challenge the Food Police
7. Cope with Your Emotions with Kindness
8. Respect Your Body
9. Movement—Feel the Difference
10. Honor Your Health—Gentle Nutrition

(Tribole & Resch, 2025)

"Intuitive Eaters march to their inner hunger signals and eat whatever they choose without experiencing guilt or an ethical dilemma."

—Evelyn Tribole, MS, RDN and Elyse Resch, MS, RDN,
Intuitive Eating, 4th Edition

No rules, no guilt, no shame.
Sounds lovely, right?

Yeah, but... aren't some foods good and some bad?

Nope. This is a privileged mindset. Some folks only have access to food you would call "bad." Regardless of it being demonized, it still sustains life. Food is food.

Sure, different foods have different nutritional qualities, but that doesn't make them good or bad. And it doesn't make a particular food right for you. For example, avocado can increase histamine production. Does that make it bad? It's largely hailed as a superfood and "good" fat. But if you have a serious histamine intolerance, then it's probably not great for you.[8]

A foundational skill of intuitive eating is body attunement: becoming tuned in to, trusting, and responding to your body's signals.

Good/bad judgment around food gets in the way of body attunement. Have you ever been out to eat and gotten the "healthy" alternative to what you wanted and then felt dissatisfied? Maybe you wanted a burger but ate a salad instead and then went through the drive-through on the way home. Letting go of good/bad judgment around food allows you to learn what you really want or need and enjoy, start using the power of choice with food, and find deeper satisfaction.

Yeah, but... if I don't have any rules around food, I'll eat everything in sight!

Nope. And... yeah, maybe. First off, that candy bar that makes your mouth water will lose its shininess when you can have it anytime. You know how after a few days of eating gas station snacks and fast food on a road trip, you start craving a home-cooked meal? Eventually, your body will tell you it'd like more balance. But that does require a level of body attunement.

Sooo, yeah, depending on your starting level of restriction, and your level of disconnection from your body, you might eat in a way that doesn't feel great. The answer still isn't restriction and re-entering the restrict/binge/self-hate cycle, or just constantly feeling bad about yourself. The answer is removing the barriers to getting in tune with your body (I cover body attunement in Chapter 6).

---

8. Don't get me wrong, I love avocado. Here's an avocado toast tip to redeem myself for saying hard things about avocados: sprinkle everything bagel seasoning on top—it's a magical combo.

Yeah, but... if I don't have rules, I will eat "too much" and get fat.

What is "too much?" I don't believe there is such a thing. This is an arbitrary amount that, in your head, isn't acceptable. Maybe you mean you ate beyond fullness, but sometimes your body is suppressing your fullness signals and increasing your appetite to make you eat "enough"—especially when you don't eat enough all day long. This is called primal hunger. Other times, when you say, "too much," you might mean you ate seconds, or more than a "serving size," or three cookies. See? Arbitrary.

The wording "too much" diminishes your body's wisdom, the myriads of reasons we need or want to eat, and the impact of restriction. Each time you shame yourself for eating "too much," you're reinforcing diet culture lies and adding shame and stress to your body. And shame increases your likelihood of eating "too much." Again, we're done with that.

Maybe you will gain weight, especially after years of restriction and avoiding many (tasty) foods. But again, fear of gaining weight or "getting fat" is anti-fat bias in full force. There's nothing wrong with gaining weight or being fat. It's a number on the scale. That number doesn't have to dictate your life. But it's important to recognize having a fat body makes some people, especially those with intersecting marginalized identities, physically less safe. Be sure to read Chapter 10 for more nuance here.

Your body is wise and doing exactly what it needs to do under the conditions it's been through. *It's time to build trust with your body.*

> "I like to refer to my body as my earth suit. There's no judgment of how big or small it is. My body's changing, but it's always been changing. And now it's at a different stage of its life. When I listen intently to my body, it tells me what its wants and needs are. And I nourish it to keep it healthy."
>
> **—MH, an awesome client**

Keep reading, but in the meantime, grab a journal and do some reflecting. Start with asking yourself these questions (be curious and do your best to let go of any self-judgment):

- What am I afraid will happen if I let go of food rules? If I stop judging food as good or bad? If I stop demonizing food?
- Why don't I trust myself to choose foods that are right for me?
- If I don't trust myself because I've eaten in a way that feels out of control, what's contributing to eating in that way?
- If I don't trust myself because I've gained weight, where did I get the message that being heavier means I'm not trustworthy?
- What number on the scale am I trying to force my body to conform to? Why?
- What number on the scale am I afraid of? Why?
- Where did those numbers come from?
- What does my number on the scale (or pants size) mean to me right now?
- How does this meaning influence my feelings about myself?
- Do I want that number to influence me in this way?

Give yourself some time to sit with your reflections. What was painful? What was surprising? Remember that much of this is deeply informed by diet culture. No self-judgment over your answers.

When Freedom Isn't Freeing

Back to the idea of no rules, no guilt, no shame... While freedom from food restriction is important and can feel great, it can also feel scary. In letting go of restriction, you may have eaten in a way that felt out of control or even unsafe. Consequently, you may have given up on the idea of intuitive eating.

Maybe you've tried intuitive eating, or maybe you haven't, but before working with me, many of my clients had the following experience trying it.

The intuitive eating messaging conveys that restriction is a big part of the problem, and clients are told to simply allow all foods, to give themselves "unconditional permission" to eat.

Unconditional permission to eat, also known as permissive eating, includes:

- eating when you're hungry, even if your preferred foods aren't available (for example, if you feel better when you include protein for breakfast but are at a meeting and there are only donuts and muffins)
- allowing yourself to eat any food
- eating for reasons other than hunger

After hearing about the concept of intuitive eating, folks may go on to eat everything that has been "off-limits"—often to an extreme. For many, this naturally slows down after a while, and they're able to start eating in a way that's more in tune with their bodies. But others get stuck eating in a way that feels out of control or haphazard, frequently eat beyond fullness, or mostly eat food that doesn't support them feeling well. This pendulum swing, from restricting to eating everything, leads to them feeling like intuitive eating is unsafe and like they can't trust themselves. This is due to confirmation bias. You've been told you can't trust yourself, so your brain is looking for evidence to confirm that bias.

One of two things happen: they either feel so out of control and terrible (mentally, emotionally, or physically) that they return to dieting (restricting), or they feel immense relief from the obsession of thinking about food and their body so much that eating whatever feels like a better alternative to restricting, but they still feel tremendous shame about the way they're engaging with food.

Eating permissively for a while can be an important resting place after restricting and focusing so much on food, but it may perpetuate body avoidance, rather than building body attunement.

There's a very popular book called *The Fuck It Diet* by Caroline Dooner. You might've even read it. While the book has some good stuff and is highly entertaining, I find the title problematic. It can give people the impression that intuitive eating is about saying "fuck it" and giving up.

If you want to just eat whatever for the rest of your life, that's totally okay. Some people prefer to stop putting their energy toward health, food, thinking about what to eat, and their bodies, or never really did to begin with. There's nothing wrong with focusing on things other than the pursuit of health.

Keep in mind that giving up on dieting (restriction) and the pursuit of thinness doesn't mean you're giving up on your health. I understand the fear of letting go of restriction, but that's likely internalized anti-fat bias rearing its ugly head. There are so many ways to focus on health that aren't about food.

If you're reading this book, chances are you've struggled with food and body image for a long time, and you'd like something more than avoidance in your relationship with food and your body. Keep reading; I'm with you.

I had a consultation with someone who felt stuck in this exact place. They said, "I'm trying to give myself permission to eat all foods, but my body doesn't feel good, and I'm gaining weight. I try to accept myself, but I really don't feel good. I feel like I've failed at intuitive eating, but I know I can't go back to dieting. I'm stuck."

I could hear the strain of shame and deep frustration in their voice. I've had many sessions with people who feel stuck in this same place of letting go of dieting (restricting) but not sure how to eat in a way that feels in alignment with their health goals. They all say some sort of variation of, "I'm trying to eat intuitively but instead I just feel like I've given up on my health and given up on who I wanted to be," or "I don't know HOW to eat intuitively. It feels impossible."

When first attempting intuitive eating, it's common to struggle with body acceptance, continually beat yourself up, and feel guilty for permissive eating.

You might've been in this situation yourself, or maybe you've been afraid of this happening, and it made you hesitant to attempt intuitive eating. So, what can you do about it?

First of all, it's important to shift your measure of success. When people diet (restrict), the standard measure of success is short-term weight loss (and we all know how that turns out—if you aren't sure, please read Appendix B, Diets Don't Work). Losing or gaining weight isn't a good measure of success for your relationship with food and your body, but people often conflate the two (this is internalized anti-fat bias). How about ease, satisfaction, joy, vitality, and acceptance as measures of success, instead?

We must prioritize mental and emotional health in addition to physical health and use better ways of determining physical health than weight.

Some non-weight related measures of success might be:

Physical health
- increased stamina/energy
- blood pressure/blood sugar/cholesterol in a good range for you
- better sleep quality
- less tension in your body
- less pain
- reduction in frequency of disordered eating behaviors

Mental and Emotional health

- less anxiety
- less preoccupation with food and/or body
- freedom from shame around food and body
- able to identify and honor emotions
- better boundaries
- greater self-compassion
- able to ask for support
- more time spent in a relaxed exploratory state
- increased overall life satisfaction
- feeling worthy or good enough

Spend a few minutes journaling or simply reflecting on your past and future measures of success.

Reflection questions:

- What were your past measures of success?
- How did they work out in the long term?
- What were they designed to do for you?
- Who benefits from the measures of success you've chased in the past?
- What have you gotten out of chasing them?
- How did they make you feel?
- What does dieting, struggling, or hating yourself justify or give you? In what ways does it hold you back?
- How would you LIKE your relationship with food and your body to be?
- What are some new measures of success you'd like to focus on?
- Why does that feel so scary?
- What might the benefits be of shifting to these new measures of success?

Try to reflect on these without self-judgment. Notice how it feels in your body when you think of past measures of success. Now, imagine measuring success in ways that better support your overall well-being. How does your body respond differently?

Another big reason people feel like they're failing when they attempt to eat intuitively is being unsure of how to decide what, when, why, and how to eat (more about this in Chapter 7) now that they're no longer basing those decisions on diet culture "shoulds." A client recently shared that the lack of rules around food left her feeling unmoored. She described feeling like she was giving up on being healthy. She admitted that it was also, in part, about giving up on striving toward looking the way she's always wanted to look.

You may experience grief around letting go of unrealistic beauty "ideals." Dismantling diet culture deeply challenges your self-image: who you want to be and how you relate to yourself, others, and the world around you. This basically causes an identity crisis. You have a new perspective, but it's a leap of faith to put it into practice. For many, diving in headfirst without clarity about how to succeed in healing is terrifying. This reminds me of Glennon Doyle's description in *Untamed* of a cheetah being caged... You're a goddamn cheetah but have been conditioned to only trust your cage because you've been in it your whole life. We're opening the door of the cage of diet culture, and stepping out can feel dangerous.

While I agree that it's important to have freedom, eating whatever isn't really freedom for most folks. It's scary and pushes people not just to the edge of their comfort zone, but often completely out of it without enough support for getting them past this stage and into truly healing their relationship with food. It's only a stage of healing. Getting stuck there or having that stage reinforce the distrust you have for your body isn't helpful, nor does it lead to healing and feeling good about food and your body.

New clients almost always tell me they want to stop dieting (restricting), but beyond that, they want peace and freedom from obsessing—over food, eating, weight, and their bodies. They want balance and to feel good in their body so they no longer have to obsess. They want to be able to trust themselves. Just like you do.

Diets (restriction) make you feel like a failure. Diet culture and the messaging that you should look a certain way and eat perfectly sets everyone up (even people who don't diet) for impossible standards and leads to internalized shame around our relationships with food and our bodies. And, again, diets simply don't work!

Questions to contemplate:

- How has restricting made me feel like a failure?
- How have the ideas around what I "should" eat or look like caused me to try to control or manage food or my body?
- Do I think that I just needed to try harder or that it's a moral failing that caused the diet to not work?
- Even when I wasn't dieting, did the idea that I "should" diet or eat less or eat "healthier" contribute to feeling bad about myself?
- What do I think the "ideal" is? How far am I from that? How often do I feel bad about the distance between the two?[9]
- Where does that "ideal" come from?

As always, try to approach these questions with curiosity, and refrain from judging yourself for your answers. We're trying to get to the root here. It can be challenging but so worth it!

---

9. When I was a girl, I'd run though all the things I'd change about my body (if I got a magic wish from a genie in a bottle). The only thing I felt was satisfactory were my wrists. I would've changed my eyes to be bluer, my skin to be tanner, my thighs to be thinner, my butt to be rounder, my boobs to be bigger and perkier. It's so sad to see how far from good enough I felt I was.

Are You Born an Intuitive Eater?

To move away from diet culture, shame, and dissatisfaction in your relationship with food and your body—to truly heal—you have to build connection and trust with your*self* and your body. Learning how to eat in a way that's attuned to your body is key to intuitive eating and healing your relationship with food and your body, but it's extremely difficult, if not impossible, to do that if the barriers aren't addressed. The barriers to learning body attunement vary widely from person to person, but can include things like systems of oppression, shame, trauma, hypervigilance, disabilities, pain, physiological differences like sensory processing disorders, addiction to alcohol or other substances, food scarcity, and the list goes on. We'll dive into what barriers you might have and how to address them in Chapter 10. Rooting out the barriers to body attunement is necessary to heal.

A common refrain I hear from other Intuitive Eating professionals is that you're born an intuitive eater, but I disagree.[10] Most of us were born with the hardware needed to become intuitive eaters, but you need to develop the software as well.[11]

If you were put on a strict feeding schedule as an infant that wasn't attuned to your body, how might that impact your wiring? You're 100% dependent on your caregivers when you're born, and you learned from them and your environment how to relate to food.

---

10. When does a person's relationship with food and their body start? In the womb? The moment of birth? If your biological mother was restricting food while pregnant with you, what might be the result?

11. There are many systems involved in feeling hunger, fullness, and other body sensations. For example, hunger and fullness signals are partly controlled by the hypothalamus, so people with congenital malformations or damage to the hypothalamus may find it much more difficult to eat intuitively. But the fact that most people have this biology is telling: we CAN trust our bodies. Bodies are so cool!

Most babies will cry when hungry and signal that they're full (turn their head, spit it out, etc.), but intuitive eating as an adult requires much more than crying when hungry or turning away when not hungry. It's so much more challenging to learn to eat intuitively while navigating the complexities of food and diet culture.

Ideally, you learn body attunement from your bonded caregivers, through them really seeing you and responding to your cues. Then they needed to show you how to attune to your body's cues yourself. But you may have been taught to ignore your body's signals instead of listening to them. Or worse, you may have learned it wasn't safe to listen to your body's signals (gaslighting).

Were you ever told you had to sit at the table until you finished your plate? Forced to eat more bites or eat food that made you gag? Were you chastised for wanting sweets? Did chores/work come first, and you could only eat when you were finished?

Did people tell you to stop crying when you were upset? Did someone get angry with you for showing emotions like fear, sadness, or excitement? Did you feel unheard or unseen as a child? These are non-food related ways that we're taught to push away our bodily experience, that we can't trust what we feel, or that our needs aren't important. We learn through our experiences.

> *It's NOT your fault.*

Need for Body Attunement and Learning to Drive

I think of learning how to eat intuitively and building body attunement like driving a car. While I hate using car analogies for bodies (you aren't a machine, you're a human), in this case, the analogy works, so bear with me.

If you had never been in a car or taught anything about what a car does or how it works, driving one would be VERY difficult, if not impossible. If you grew up on a farm and were taught how to drive tractors at a young age, you'd probably pick up driving a car with ease. For most of us, there's a big learning curve with driving. You have to be taught and then practice it for months and months before you're given a license. Then, it still takes a while to become capable and comfortable. It can take years to become a really good driver. But after gaining experience and muscle memory, you can drive pretty much on autopilot, unless you're driving in difficult circumstances and you need to pay more attention.[12]

Intuitive eating and body attunement are like that; we all have slightly different physiology, but most of us can learn to be attuned and intuitive eaters, if shown how (with practice). This is an important distinction. You can't expect yourself to just know how. It takes time, focus, and compassion to learn and develop the skill. It may feel hard and uncomfortable, but it's totally possible to learn at any age.

Taking the analogy further, there may be other reasons you struggle to learn to drive based on your abilities, your environment, or the things people have told you about driving. If you experienced someone constantly telling you how dangerous driving is, you might get such bad anxiety while driving that you can't focus. If your nervous system is very dysregulated, driving would be more difficult. If you have difficulties with sensory or motor processing, you might need to develop additional skills to be able to drive safely.

If someone told you that you're bad at driving, you can't trust yourself on the road, or there's something wrong with you, then developing the confidence to drive would be hard. If you have

---

12. Thank god for driver's ed; teaching my daughter and stepson to drive was T E R R I F Y I N G! But we got through it with only a few little incidents, lol. But my neck was so sore...

physical or cognitive differences, it might be impossible to drive, or you may need a vehicle modified to fit your needs. And if you aren't in a place of financial privilege, you might not be able to access the necessities to make it work.

Similarly, learning the basic skill of body attunement is foundational for eating intuitively. If you've never developed the habit of noticing when you're full because you were taught to clean your plate, if you were actively taught to disregard your body signals, or that those signals are bad, how can you expect that you'll just know how to eat intuitively?

> *You can't.*

And that's the problem. The *barriers* to learning how to tune in to your body's signals need to be addressed. You have to learn how to eat intuitively, which takes time, support, and perseverance.

If you experience challenges with body attunement (many people do), the simplified intuitive eating messaging could contribute to you feeling like there's something wrong with you because you can't just "tune in" to your body and live happily ever after. There is nothing wrong with you. Your struggles and challenges make sense.

> *You are not broken.*

Healing is possible! Here's one client's experience with healing in her own words.

"Before working with Tiffany, I lived in a constant state of frustration with my relationship with food and with my body. I was always looking for the next thing that would click for me and make it easier. Over the last three decades, I've tried every type of restriction, workout plan, new fad, or established diet out there.

Whole30, paleo, WeightWatchers, a nutritionist, Noom, *Eat Like a Tree*,[13] intermittent fasting, food journals, no sugar, no meat, no fun. I've done all of them. Even [restricted food] while training to run over a dozen half-marathons, a marathon, and two triathlons. I've abused exercise as well. I never felt satisfied or peaceful with what I was doing. I've been up and down the scale. I always lived in a state of hypervigilance about food. I've also been full of shame and disappointment with my eating and with what I deemed a failure on my part to figure it out and be done with "this problem."

I started to realize that *the problem wasn't with me. There is nothing wrong with me. I was setting myself up for failure time and time again because diets don't work.*

I've learned how to listen to my body. I've learned that my emotions and thoughts about food were coming from a place of deep shame about my history with food and assigning value and worth to things that have nothing to do with me. I am so much more than any number on a scale or any smaller pants size. Tiffany has

---

13. Yes, there's a book called *How to Eat Like a Tree: Unearthing the Moderate Eater in You* by Dara Boland. It's supposed to show you how to be a "moderate eater" and "maintain a natural weight," like trees do, I guess??

While trying to learn more about it via Google, I found a Quora question that illustrates how extreme our collective food issues are. Someone asked, "Can I survive on eating only trees, rocks and grass?" First of all, NO, second of all, NO, third of all, WHYYYYYY??? Please, NEVER eat rocks.

helped me dismantle the self-destructive thinking and restrictive/ policing thoughts I've developed over decades of negative self-talk, restriction, and adherence to societal norms based on all the wrong things—my body shape has nothing to do with who I am as a person and with my value and worth in society. I've learned that my hunger deserves to be honored. I've learned that my voice should be heard and not stifled and stuffed down. I've learned that it's okay to have boundaries and to cherish my thoughts and opinions. I've learned that trusting myself is the most important thing I can do. Furthermore, even though it's hard, trusting myself is the only way to go. It's worth the effort it takes to get there.

I'm able to eat meals with my family and not feel left out or stressed out or overwhelmed by analyzing everything. I finish a meal and move on to the next activity instead of obsessing about what I ate or how it did or did not fit into some model someone else gave me about how I "am supposed to eat." Food restriction is not a way to get to a happy place. Food s not the enemy. Food is food. It's meant to be enjoyed and it's good to feel satisfied with the food you're eating. I'm able to see my needs more objectively and to question and be curious about eating behavior instead of judging it and feeling bad about it.

I'm learning how to be a kind friend to myself and to cherish what my body does for me and to be proud of who I am based on my personality and relationships, not on the size of my hips. I love that I have gotten off the roller coaster of the diet industry. I have no intention of returning to that world. I'm finding my way with this new relationship with food and more importantly with myself. It's incredible to me how much of my mental energy was tied up with thoughts about food, exercise, body image, and disappointment or fear about some aspect of those things. Now I have so much more bandwidth for my big, wonderful life. Peace with food is possible."

—SB, a wonderful client

Chapter Three

Discovering the Solution: Attachment Theory

It's so funny the way life experiences can feel like falling on your face at first but turn out to be exactly what you need. And sometimes, they even lead to something magical.

After healing my relationship with food and my body, I was so much more in tune with my needs and desires. As I started honoring those needs and desires, I became more and more empowered to build the life that I wanted and that supported me best. I left my job at the hospital that was draining my soul. I left a seventeen-year relationship.[14] I started living a life that felt aligned with my values.

When I started dating again and got into a serious relationship, I discovered I had an anxious/preoccupied relationship pattern with

---

14. My was-band (a term I adopted from a client that I like better than ex-husband) was a good man, and we had a nice life, but it wasn't what I needed to live fully. It was so hard to break my loyal-to-a-fault self-narrative and hurt people by leaving just to give myself what I needed. As painful as that was, it was absolutely the right choice. I've never regretted the decision. You are the only person living your life. Do what's right for you.

someone I cared deeply for. I was constantly worried about our relationship, overthinking, and afraid of losing my partner ALL THE TIME. It was disrupting my life. It was PAINFUL to be so anxious. It made me feel like there was something wrong with me.

I've always been very growth-focused, and this new relationship challenge was no exception. I hated that I wanted to control and manage every little thing and that it was taking up so much of my mental and emotional energy (much like I used to feel in my relationship with food). I have important shit to do with my life and didn't want any relationship to derail me, not to mention that it was making the relationship suck, and it just felt miserable.

I dove into everything I could find about how to have a healthy relationship. I discovered the book *Polysecure* by Jessica Fern. I knew within a few pages that it was exactly what I needed. It turns out there's nothing wrong with me; I just had some unhealed attachment issues. I highly recommend reading *Polysecure* (even if you aren't polyamorous). The author's way of explaining attachment theory and how to build a more secure relationship is so approachable.

While on a long walk trying to sort out some difficult feelings, listening to *Polysecure* (the author's voice is super soothing), an idea literally stopped me in my tracks. In the chapter on becoming securely attached with self, Fern shares how there are different ways to begin doing this work. You can start with your relationship with self or relationships with others first. Regardless of the order, it's important to focus on your relationship with yourself in addition to your relationships with others for deeper healing.

While I still had relationship attachment work to do, I realized I had already become securely attached with myself... *through healing my relationship with food and my body!*

In healing my relationship with food and my body, I found a solid foundation rooted in knowing my value and worth isn't tied to external things like appearance, that I deserve to make myself the priority, and that I can trust myself. I was securely attached with myself, and now it was time to work to become securely attached in my relationships with others.

I realized the work I had done to heal, and was supporting clients in, had been attachment work all along. I simply hadn't had the language for it.

It's so common for clients to come to a session feeling shame about their eating behaviors. I encourage them to let go of judgment around the behaviors. Judgment breeds shame and blocks change. With compassion, we get curious about the circumstances surrounding the behavior, the client's thoughts, feelings, and what sensations are present in their body. We follow the threads. Inevitably, they lead us to something a caregiver or significant person(s) said or did growing up (or even last week). These experiences left them feeling like they weren't good enough in some way—aka shame.

All of that shame, those childhood and life experiences, are drivers for your eating patterns and body relationship. Shame also moves you further and further from your connection with yourself and your body. This is why we have to look at the relationship with food, your body, and yourself.

Food + Attachment

Your food and body relationships developed from the moment you were born (likely even before that) as you bonded with caregivers and began learning from your environment.

We're born with inherent instinctual desires for food and connection. We can't live without relationships, and we can't live without food. They're integral parts of being human. When you were a baby, someone had to feed you and care for you so you would survive. Infants can literally die of loneliness, and even as adults, we're more likely to die prematurely if we lack social connection.

Connection is a hardwired survival need. The connection or bond you formed with your caregivers as an infant is referred to as "attachment." How you were nourished and cared for impacts how you attached to your caregivers and your overall development. Being fed and held in response to crying gives you the message that your caregiver is tuned in to your signals. You learn that you're safe, and most importantly, that you MATTER.

> "The central theme of attachment theory is that primary caregivers who are available and responsive to an infant's needs allow the child to develop a sense of security. The infant knows that the caregiver is dependable, which creates a secure base for the child to then explore the world."
> —Very Well Mind, 2025

Food, relationships, security, and self-worth are deeply intertwined. The experience of being fed as an infant has a huge impact on how you attach to others and your attachment with your*self*. As you grew up and began to understand you're separate and autonomous from your caregivers, you developed relationships with your*self*, with your body, and with food.

> *You have a **direct relationship** with food, expressed through patterns and behaviors.*

Many of your food patterns were wired in at a young age and are reactions (or rather, responses) to those early childhood experiences. Those life experiences, informed by your relationships with others (and our collective culture), along with your physiology, genetics, and disposition/personality, create your food and body attachment style.

While most of us have the structures in place to develop wiring for a secure attachment with others, ourselves, food, and our bodies, we're dependent on our caregivers to get our needs met. If your needs weren't *seen* and *met* often enough, it creates an attachment wound. The response to those wounds is to develop an insecure attachment style and, accordingly, behavior strategies to survive.

For example, a baby or child who's forced to eat regardless of hunger or fullness signals may grow up to be avoidant of food or consistently eat beyond fullness. If you were put on a restrictive diet at a young age, you may sneak and hide food. If you were neglected as a baby or child, you may try to ignore your own needs to be less of a burden. As an adult, you perpetuate the survival strategies and behavior patterns you developed unconsciously along the way. This can create pain, shame, confusion, and difficulties in relationship with your*self*, your body, food, and with others.

This is at the core of why diets never work. Trying to restrict, control, or manage your way to a healthy relationship with food and your body *doesn't heal attachment wounds and leads to even more anxiety, preoccupation, or avoidance.*

Unhealed attachment wounds can also be the gap between feeling like a failure with intuitive eating and finding peace with food. It's so much more complex than simply letting go of diet culture and listening to your body. You probably don't know how to listen to your body.

My clients were coming to me with a disconnection from their body, deep shame, and self-hatred. These are attachment wounds with your*self*. Many of these wounds go back decades. Some go all the way back to infancy. To heal these wounds, we must go beyond intuitive eating to untangle the underlying issues. This is why I created the food and body attachment model.

Through this new lens, we can see any unhealed wounds and barriers to having the relationship with food and your body that you really want. *You can heal these wounds.* Many of these wounds are rooted in low self-worth. If you don't feel good enough as you are, you've likely developed survival strategies such as constantly wanting to change or fix yourself,[15] attempting to control food, ignoring your body's signals, or putting others above yourself. If you were told you can't trust your body's signals or that there's something wrong with your body, it likely won't feel safe to listen to and honor your body's signals, to follow your own internal compass.

To let go of diet culture, you have to heal your attachment wounds, change your sense of self-worth, and discover how to feel safe listening to your body's signals. To do that, we have to go way back to the experiences you had and messages you received as a child and throughout your life.

This reflection is the piece that's missing from intuitive eating for some folks. This is why some people feel it doesn't relate to them, and why others feel like failures when they try to eat intuitively. We must go deeper and delve into how and why we relate to food and our bodies the way we do, and we can do this through understanding our attachment style. Learning your food and body attachment style, which we will do in Chapter 4, will help bridge the gap. It'll help you understand why you've struggled and what to do about your unique challenges so you can finally have the relationship with food and your body that you want. You can have peace, satisfaction, and ease. You can build a trusting relationship with your body and food can become joyful nurturance.

---

15. Reminder: you're not broken and don't need to be fixed.

*You can be
friends with
your body.*

Thoughts on My Body

"The purpose of your body is relationship with yourself, others, and the Divine."
—Amanda Martinez Beck, *The Fat Dispatch*

After years of struggle, I finally healed my relationship with my body. While I say "healed," I don't love the term because it implies a previous brokenness, and then a destination of "healed." Instead of being broken, I was wounded. Instead of a destination, *healed* is a practice I've learned; a practice of caring for my body, exactly as it is, rather than trying to fix or control it. From a place of earned secure attachment with my body, I am empowered. Today, my most treasured possession is my body.

I've worked to develop a deep connection and trust with my body. My body has served me well. It allows me to smile and to bring a smile to others' faces, and it has carried me through all of the challenges and joys in my life. It's the only thing I will possess for my entire life; it's my longest and most fulfilling relationship. My body is the place I am always. It's where I belong.

If this sounds like the kind of relationship you'd like with your body, I'd love nothing more than to help support you in your healing. It's possible, keep reading.

I believe in you.

How Do You Relate to Food?
The Four Food and Body Attachment Styles

According to attachment theory, there are four distinct styles of attachment that folks can develop as babies and children that inform all of your relationships. Not only do those experiences impact you as child, but they continue to impact you and drive how you show up in your relationships in adulthood

The four attachment styles are:
- secure or earned secure
- dismissive avoidant
- anxious avoidant (also referred to as fearful/disorganized)
- preoccupied/anxious

Dismissive avoidant, anxious avoidant, and preoccupied/anxious are considered insecure attachment styles. The relationship attachment styles *can also be used to describe how you relate to food and your body.* The food and body attachment model shows how your patterns with food are developed out of attachment needs.

If you have an insecure attachment style, you'll tend to either obsess over food and your body, rigidly try to control food or body, ignore food or body, or fluctuate somewhere in between.

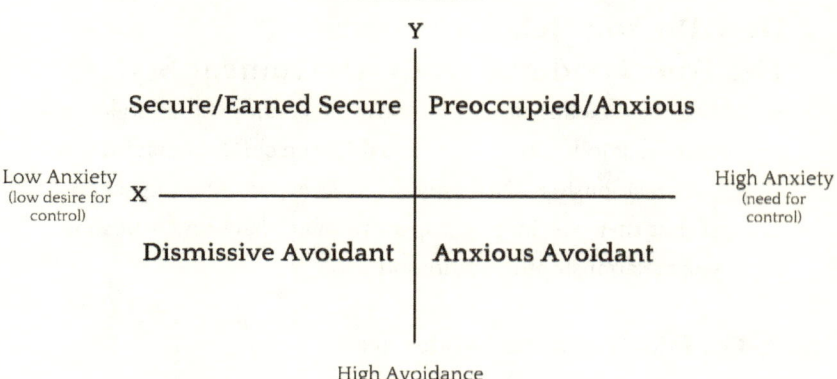

This graph represents the four attachment styles. Notice the X and Y axis. The X axis represents the level of *felt* anxiety around food and your body, and the Y axis represents the level of avoidance of food and of your body's signals/needs, low to high.

Secure Types

Secure or Earned Secure Attachment = Low Anxiety + Low Avoidance

This is the least common attachment style I see when people come to a consultation with me. They already feel good in their relationship with food and body. They typically don't feel the need to get additional guidance. People with this attachment style were taught to appreciate and trust their body. They relate to food and movement as nurturance. They experience ease with food.

If you weren't supported in developing secure attachment as a child, you can still become secure by working on it. This attachment style is called *earned* secure. The goal of this book is to help you come to a place of earned secure attachment with food and your body (it's possible, and it's awesome!).

Insecure Types

Preoccupied/Anxious Attachment =
High Anxiety + *Low Avoidance*

This is the most common attachment style I see in my practice. If you have a preoccupied/anxious style of attachment, you're thinking about food and your body most of the time (most clients with this attachment style report thinking about food or body 80% of the time). You're almost always trying to figure out how to control or manage food and your body to achieve some "ideal" or beating yourself up for not having met that "ideal" already.

Anxious Avoidant Attachment =
High Anxiety + *High Avoidance*

This is the second-most common attachment style of people coming to me for support. If you have a more anxious avoidant attachment style, you're likely very disconnected from food and your body in a very rigid or controlled way. You likely try to avoid eating, don't want to be dependent on food, or exercise intensely in a way that isn't tuned in to your body. Eating with others increases your anxiety, so you typically avoid it.

Dismissive Avoidant Attachment =
Low (Felt) Anxiety + *High Avoidance*

This is the third most common attachment style I see in my practice, although, it's less common for someone with this attachment style to decide to continue to work with me beyond consultation. One of the reasons for this is due to an avoidance tendency and the low-felt anxiety (think *head in the sand*). If you want to throw this book away, you may have avoidant attachment, but I'm so glad you're here.

If you have a dismissive avoidant food and body attachment style, you eat in ways that are very disconnected from your body's signals, eating whatever, whenever. You likely wait to eat until your hunger signals knock you over the head. Food ends up being an afterthought. You might use food to regulate your nervous system, soothe, or feel comfort. You may also use it for entertainment.

> *You are not broken.*

If you lean more toward an insecure attachment style with food, know that your relationship with food isn't bad, and you aren't broken. There is nothing wrong with you if you struggle with food; it's simply the way you've survived.

Most people have some characteristics from each, or at least some characteristics from more than one style, but tend to lean more toward one. You can have different attachment styles in different relationships. For example, you may be preoccupied with food but more avoidant with your body, or more anxious avoidant with a lover, but more dismissive avoidant with a parent.

As we delve deeper into the food and body attachment styles, keep in mind that discovering your style is only important in understanding your current relationship with food and *to guide your discovery of what you need to move toward the relationship you really want.* There's no *right* way to be. Again, you developed your attachment style and subsequent behavior strategies as a small child based on your lived experience to help you survive. You're alive, so clearly, it worked! At least, it worked for you on some level: here you are, having survived up to this point.

The next chapter is all about the different attachment styles from the lens of the food and body attachment model. I'll introduce you to four clients. For privacy purposes, each client represented is an amalgamation of different people I've worked with, not a direct representation of one actual client.

Watch for your past patterns and what you most closely identify with at this point in your life. I'll share more about barriers to secure attachment and how to become more secure—our ultimate goal—in later chapters. Please note: I don't focus much on these clients' body types because you can have any type of challenge with food regardless of your size.

Fortunately, now that you know it's possible to have the relationship with food and your body that you really want, you can learn how. Knowing is half the battle![16]

---

16. I know this reference won't make sense to everyone… but true to my GenX identity, I couldn't not.

Chapter Four

Food and Body Attachment Styles

I developed the food and body attachment styles to help guide you in understanding where you are now and how to move toward the relationship with food that you truly want. It isn't the be-all, end-all. There are many paths to healing. My deep desire is that this model will shift the way we think about food, our bodies, and health, enabling more people to find relief from the pain of struggling in their food and body relationships. I hope it'll continue to evolve as people consider this lens and work to expand upon it so even more folks will benefit. When I read *Emergent Strategy* by adrienne maree brown, I loved how she framed her work as a contribution and welcomed collaboration. So refreshing. This speaks to my sense of community, valuing others and their ideas. I personally found support in so many places, and I wanted to gather them here for you. This is why I've included so many resources throughout the book.

In the same spirit, this model is a starting point, a living, breathing concept. It's meant to grow and evolve.

You are the authority on you, so if something doesn't resonate, leave it. If I've left something out, add it. This is only a map, but YOU have the compass (hint: it's your body).

Secure/Earned Secure: "I Enjoy Food"
Low anxiety (low need for control) + low avoidance

Sophia (she/her)[17] came to me because of her love of food and interest in health. As she recounts her relationship with food as a child, she gets a pleasant faraway look on her face and relaxes into her chair. She tells me she had a happy childhood. Her mother was very loving and always cooked for their family. Her dad wasn't around as much because he worked a lot, but he was kind and encouraging. They always ate meals together as a family. She wasn't pushed to eat foods she didn't like and really enjoyed her mom's home-cooked meals. She says she loves all kinds of foods, even veggies.

As an adult, Sophia became more adventurous with food and likes to have a lot of variety. With her busy career, she tends to eat out more often than she'd like to, and she worries it isn't healthy. Another concern is occasionally "overeating" (eating past full), but she tells me she doesn't beat herself up too much about that because it happens most often when she gets overly hungry, or when she's at a family gathering and the food is just so yummy.

Her other concern is that she's always hearing about intermittent fasting, keto, and other diets, and wonders if she's doing enough for her health. When I ask about her health, she tells me she feels pretty good overall and her blood pressure and labs are all in the normal range, but she's in the "ob*se" (bogus) BMI category and her doctor told her to lose weight. She has acceptance over her body size, and considers herself to be very body-positive, but again worries some that her weight isn't ideal for her health.

Sophia loves to exercise, especially in dance classes, yoga, and lifting weights. She had a membership to a body-positive gym and

---

17. My dear friend and amazing anxiety coach Katherine Kozioziemski shared with me that she'd named the secure part of herself "Sophia" because it means wisdom. I love that so much.

loved going there to take classes. Sadly, it closed due to the pandemic. She hasn't found a routine with exercise since it was disrupted in 2020, even though she has the equipment she needs at home. She wistfully says that the best part of the gym was connection—being social in the classes and the motivation and support from the trainers.

Sophia has a mostly secure food and body attachment style. She was raised in a safe and loving environment where food was consistently provided. Her autonomy around food choices was respected. This helped Sophia develop body attunement, allowing her to trust her hunger and fullness signals, and her likes and dislikes. When we're securely attached, we can take more risk; as she grew up, she became more adventurous with food. She enjoys exercise for how it makes her feel, not because of a "should."

Sophia enjoys food, eats in an attuned way, and cares for herself well. Her concerns are largely due to exposure to anti-fat bias, diet culture messages, weight stigma (especially at the doctor), and the false messages that you'll be unhealthy if you eat out a lot and if you're in an "overweight" (bogus) BMI category. Sophia would benefit from limiting her exposure to the outside messages of diet culture and actively rejecting them. She has a secure foundation with food and her body—those outside messages only cause her to doubt herself. She'd benefit from a Health at Every Size® provider who helps her focus on health markers rather than weight. Going forward, building deeper self-trust will be key for her overall well-being and life satisfaction.

Secure attachment characteristics:

- in *relationship* with food and body—connected but not overly anxious
- attuned to hunger/fullness and other body sensations and signals

- prioritizing yourself
- eating regularly and well
- able to enjoy food
- attending to underlying health issues, needs, and emotions
- able to receive food from others
- using structure as a supportive tool, with flexibility
- experiencing ease with food
- enjoying movement for the mental and physical benefits, not because of a "should"
- holding no moral judgment of yourself or others around health or size
- recognizing and rejecting the social construct that beauty is tied to value
- recognizing that you're deserving of pleasure at any size, age, or appearance
- accepting and appreciating your body now and as it changes

Preoccupied: "Food Controls Me"
High anxiety (need for control) + low avoidance
(This was me before finding Intutive Eating)

Penny (she/they) came to me a few years into recovery from alcohol, worried about "emotional eating, bingeing, and sugar cravings." They wondered aloud if they had "a food addiction" and are "sick of thinking about food so much and hating myself." Penny tells me she's worried she just replaced one addiction for another.

When I asked Penny about their relationship with food as a child, she recounted that her mom first put her on a diet at around age eight. They recall sneaking food often and using all their babysitting money on snacks at the corner market. Penny was a competitive swimmer in middle and high school, but her mom still frequently told her to watch what she ate. In college, they restricted food in an attempt to stay thin.

After having children, Penny struggled more and more with dieting. She'd diet, "fall off the wagon," binge, feel terrible about herself, and try dieting once again. Penny was always trying the newest diet, thinking this would be the one that would finally work for good. But the pattern was always the same: she'd lose about 20 pounds and then gain them back, plus some. When Penny started drinking heavily, they'd routinely drink and eat late into the night, after the kids went to bed. Describing this pattern to me, a look of shame clouded their face.

After getting sober, they noticed even more obsession with food and intense food cravings. Once again, they tried dieting and felt like they were just hitting their head against a wall. She came to me desperate to break free of the struggle.

Penny has a primarily preoccupied food and body attachment style. They're very focused on food, always trying to control and manage food in an attempt to fix their issues with food. There's a long-term pattern of restrict/binge/shame cycles.

They'd benefit from outside support from a somatic coach or therapist to dismantle shame and heal the underlying trauma from being made to feel they weren't good enough as a child and young adult. Additionally, rather than focusing on weight loss as the measure of success, Penny needs to redefine success as growth in intuitive eating skills, building body attunement, and development of self-trust.

A note about sugar addiction: there are many reasons that struggling with sugar cravings is NOT like alcohol or substance use disorder or physiological addiction to those substances. It doesn't change your neurobiology in the same way. There are many reasons you might be craving sugar (food restriction, poor gut flora, low neurotransmitters, nervous system dysregulation, nutrient deficiencies, not eating enough during the day, the list goes on) but labeling yourself a sugar addict only increases shame and does nothing to help shift the underlying issues.

Preoccupied characteristics:

- chronic dieting, restricting/bingeing pattern
- high focus on food, meal/food planning
- food and body checking taking up a ton of mental space
- having many "shoulds" or rules around food
- using food to soothe
- becoming upset if unable to maintain rigid rituals and routine
- having shame around "failing"
- constantly talking about food or bodies
- Last Supper eating (finishing off food so it won't be tempting in the future)
- possible past or current experiences with food scarcity (not having enough food may lead to intense food preoccupation)
- hiding food or secretive eating due to shame
- exhibiting signs of orthorexia

Anxious Avoidant: "I Control Food and My Body"
High anxiety (need for control) + high avoidance

Austin (he/him) comes to see me reluctantly. He'd scheduled a couple of times and then rescheduled. But finally, a couple months after his first try, he made it to our consultation. I can see he's feeling really anxious. He tells me all in one breath how he's been severely restricting food for many years.

When I ask Austin about his childhood, he says things were difficult at home. His parents fought all the time and being at the table felt like torture. He'd do whatever he could to get out of there as often as possible. When his parents divorced, he spent a lot of time with his grandmother who was really strict and forced him to eat but then told him he had to watch his weight. When his mom got remarried, his stepdad was terrible, and he was scared to be home. He moved out on his own at 17.

Austin tells me he doesn't want to have to depend on food and actively ignores his hunger signals, and he often doesn't even feel hungry anymore. Over his adult life, he's had different patterns around food. Mostly, he restricts and eats very little, but sometimes he has large binge episodes and occasionally purges. But these patterns remain consistent—his avoidance and restriction of food alongside ignoring his body signals. He says he's terrified of gaining weight. He lifts weights and runs daily.

Austin explains he doesn't like to eat with others because it stresses him out. He's afraid they'll scrutinize what he's eating or notice that he isn't eating much. He almost always prepares the same meals and gets really upset if something gets in the way of his routines. He'd like to travel with a volunteer organization, but he's afraid it'd be too hard to manage his food situation and his need for many hours of exercise per day. He noticed he's getting sick more often and people are starting to comment that he looks pale and thin.

When we talk about what he'd like his relationship with food to be like, he says he really doesn't know, but he's worried that the restriction is too hard on his body. He also says he'd like to finally feel free of the need to control food.

Austin has an anxious avoidant relationship with food and his body. He avoids eating whenever possible and ignores his hunger and fullness signals. He's extremely disconnected from his body. He has a high level of anxiety about food and body, and he's visibly struggling to regulate his nervous system.

Austin would benefit from getting support from an eating disorder recovery team, including a doctor, and other trained professionals, such as a dietitian, therapist, coach, etc. He'll likely need to do in-depth processing around his childhood trauma, find ways to regulate his nervous system beyond exercise, relearn how to eat consistently, and learn to feel safe enough to trust his body's signals (body attunement).

Note about eating disorders: any gender can experience an eating disorder, and in any body size. It's so important to increase this awareness because eating disorders have a high mortality rate and can be such an isolating experience.

Anxious avoidant characteristics:

- extreme restriction
- has an active eating disorder: anorexia, bulimia, purging (reminder, anyone of any size can experience any type of eating disorder, including men)
- feeling unsafe around taking in nourishment
- exercise dependent (or extreme amount of exercising)
- experiences high shame
- extreme privacy surrounding challenges with food
- highly controlling around food intake
- possible need for intense structure or control in other areas of life
- isolation from others
- doesn't want to be physically dependent on food
- disregarding of hunger signals
- has intense fear of gaining weight
- disconnected from body to the point of dissociation (doesn't feel safe in body)
- may have digestive challenges that make it uncomfortable to eat or hard to digest food

Dismissive Avoidant:
"I Don't Even Want to Think About Food"
Low (felt) anxiety + high avoidance

Devin (they/them) came to me concerned about their health and weight. They tell me they hate dieting, or rather, can never stick to it, even for a day. They "just eat whatever" but don't feel great and think they should do something about it.

When I ask Devin about what food and meals were like in their childhood home, they get a disgruntled look on their face. When they were young, their parents would cook the grossest food and force them to sit at the table all night if they didn't eat it. They said food often made them gag so it was a horrible experience. When they were 10, their parents got a divorce, and their mom became depressed. Devin had to learn to fend for themselves. They mostly made ramen or mayo and cheese sandwiches.

Now Devin primarily eats the same things all the time, mainly quick and easy meals like cereal, Top Ramen, and chips. They don't like to prepare food and feel confined when their partner wants to meal plan; they want to be able to just eat whatever they're in the mood for. They have an aversion to meat, fish, several types of veggies, and many food textures.

Sometimes they go all day without eating and become very hungry. They end up eating so much that they feel sick and need to take medication for it. Oftentimes, they leave the house to run errands in the afternoon and realize they hadn't yet eaten that day, so they end up eating out a lot. Other times, they'll find themself snacking all day, typically when they're bored. They want to exercise more, but get distracted, and when they do remember, it's hard to get motivated.

Devin also shares that as a pre-teen, they were very uncomfortable with the changes happening with their body and were embarrassed when people pointed out those changes. It didn't feel like their body fit the way they viewed themselves. They didn't really have any support from their parents or a safe place to explore their gender. They felt that experience caused a lot of painful feelings of self-hatred and disconnection from their body. They're feeling more comfortable with their body now that they have a supportive therapist, started hormone therapy, and have started to shift their outward gender expression to what feels right for them rather than the gender they were assigned at birth.

They say, "I want to feel better, and I do want to take better care of my body, but I don't really want to have to think much about food."

Devin has a dismissive/avoidant food and body attachment style. They're laissez-faire about what and when to eat, are disconnected from their body's signals, and tend to avoid the relationship with food and their body. They don't seem to feel much anxiety about food other than feeling some "shoulds" around it, and rarely, when they do notice that they aren't feeling good, they feel shame. Their body avoidance is in part due to gender dysphoria, the anti-transgender systems of oppression, and a lack of support around their gender expression.

Devin would benefit from continued support from their therapist and finding a coach or group program where they feel safe—one that will support them in consistently looking at their relationship with food and their body. They may also benefit from being evaluated for sensory processing challenges and neurodivergence. Because of their avoidant tendencies, they'll need support so they don't go back to disconnecting from their body and the way they feel. The goal will be to create more internal safety, develop body awareness, and establish systems that support them eating regularly and well.

Dismissive avoidant characteristics:
- disconnected from hunger/fullness, may not eat all day
- not knowing what to eat, a defeatist attitude about food

- eating whatever—not in an attuned way
- avoiding structure—doesn't want to be restricted or constrained
- eating beyond fullness to the point of dissociation
- regularly using medication to avoid food discomfort (for example, Tums after meals)
- eating the same things all the time
- disliking meal planning and food prep
- self-neglectful
- may be neurodivergent[18]

Your Food and Body Attachment Style

Ready to learn your style? You can take my quiz (coachtiffanyrn. com/quiz) or use the checklists below. Keep in mind that you can't tell a person's food and body attachment style by looking at them; people in all types of bodies can have any style. No one can tell if you're securely attached based on an outside perspective, for example, you can't look at one's food choices or fitness level and know. It's all about how you're relating to food and your body. And no one fits perfectly into one box... most of us have some characteristics from each style. Again, this is simply a guide to figure out your starting point and help you find more peace and satisfaction in your relationship with food and your body.

Secure statements:
☐ I enjoy food.
☐ Sharing a meal with friends or family brings me joy.
☐ I see eating as self-care.
☐ For the most part, I eat when I'm hungry and stop when I'm full.
☐ I can be flexible in my meal plans.

---

18. Or "neurospicy," as some of my friends like to say ☺

☐ I eat regularly throughout the day.

☐ If I eat beyond fullness, I don't beat myself up about it.

☐ At times, I eat something just because I want it.

☐ When I'm going through something, I tend to seek support from others.

☐ I'm comfortable feeling my feelings.

☐ I may occasionally use food to soothe myself, but I don't beat myself up.

☐ I mostly eat food that I enjoy, and that makes me feel good.

☐ I enjoy a variety of food.

☐ I appreciate my body.

☐ I'm fairly in tune with my body and make self-care a priority.

Secure statements total: _____ **/15**

Preoccupied statements:

☐ I use food for love, connection, or comfort.

☐ I think about food, dieting, when or what I'll eat next, or meal planning *a lot.*

☐ I'm very aware of how much I'm eating.

☐ I often track meals, macros, or calories.

☐ I've done a lot of diets.

☐ I feel better about myself when I'm on a diet.

☐ Food takes up a lot of space in my brain.

☐ I feel like I'm obsessed with food.

☐ When I'm going through something, I tend to eat to soothe myself.

☐ After a binge episode, I beat myself up and try to "get back on track."

☐ Before I diet, I try to eat all the "junk" food in the house so I won't be tempted.

- [ ] I'm always talking to friends about diets and weight.
- [ ] I weigh myself to see if I'm "doing okay" or to see how "badly" I've been eating.
- [ ] I'm constantly checking my body and comparing it to others' bodies when in public.
- [ ] If people knew how I ate when alone, I'd be so embarrassed.

Preoccupied statements total: _____ **/15**

Anxious avoidant statements:

- [ ] I have to manage food.
- [ ] I don't want to depend on anything, not even food.
- [ ] I don't know what's safe to eat.
- [ ] If people knew the intimate details of my eating patterns, I'd be mortified.
- [ ] I HAVE to exercise.
- [ ] I try to eat as little as possible.
- [ ] I vacillate between eating very little and extreme bingeing.
- [ ] My relationship with food feels very chaotic—I have to keep it in control.
- [ ] I'm very uncomfortable in my body.
- [ ] The higher my stress, the more I try to manage food and exercise.
- [ ] I feel at times I'm hurting my body by bingeing or not eating.
- [ ] I often disassociate myself from my body.
- [ ] I can't talk to anyone about my issues with food.
- [ ] I want to be as small as possible.
- [ ] I'm not always honest about food with my providers.

Anxious avoidant statements total: _____ **/15**

Dismissive avoidant statements:

- ☐ I've "given up."
- ☐ I know what I "should" eat, but I just don't.
- ☐ I don't really know what to eat.
- ☐ Food just isn't that important to me.
- ☐ I don't really like new or different foods.
- ☐ I forget to eat frequently.
- ☐ I'd rather just eat the things that are easy.
- ☐ Sometimes I numb out when eating.
- ☐ I often don't notice when I'm getting overly full.
- ☐ I often need medication for my indigestion because of what or how I ate.
- ☐ I feel pretty disconnected from my body.
- ☐ I often don't know what I'm feeling.
- ☐ Food plans make me feel like I'm being controlled.
- ☐ I only want to eat what I'm in the mood for.
- ☐ I can never seem to maintain "healthy" eating habits.

Dismissive avoidant statements total: _____ **/15**

Add up the number of boxes in each section. The section with the highest score is your current attachment style. Notice other sections with 3-4+ points: this style is also part of your food and body relationship and will give you clues about your patterns. You may oscillate between a couple of different styles, or your attachment style may show up differently with food than with your body.

It's also interesting to look at life stages and styles; perhaps you had tendencies toward one style in your teen and college years versus your 40s. These patterns are fluid, meaning they can change over time, and that's great news... you can shift your relationship with food and your body to be more aligned with how you'd like it to be at any time! Ready for change? Keep reading!

Chapter Five

Soft and Sustainable Change

"What is easy is sustainable. Birds coast when they can."

—adrienne maree brown, *Emergent Strategy: Shaping Change, Changing Worlds*

Do you have the belief that change is hard? You might be thinking, *of course change is hard!* But is it? Does it always have to be? Says who? Does change have to be hard to be effective?

In what circumstances is change hard? Can you think of a time when you changed some pattern or grew in a way that felt simple or easeful?

Change simply is. We're constantly changing. It feels difficult or impossible if you aren't resourced enough (meaning you have the support, tools, and skills you need to make the changes you want). Change also doesn't work if you force it, push yourself too hard, or override your body.

It's time to approach change from a place of moving toward and building connection with your (awesome, wise, magical) self, instead of moving away from, overriding, or fighting against yourself.

Change can feel so daunting. There are layers of "shoulds," diet culture messaging, self-criticism, and misinformation about how, what, when, and why to change.

How about this mantra? "No pain, no gain." Right? Wrong.

What if change could be EASY? What if you only had to practice new tools in a way that felt good and aligned with your body? It's time to stop fighting against yourself and start working with yourself—and with your body.

Do you have the idea that you "should" change because something is wrong with you?

The mantra "if you REALLY loved yourself, you would..." is so harmful. Trying to fix yourself because you're "broken" or "bad" or "wrong" is like waging war on yourself. It'll result in pain and shame, pushing you further into anxious or avoidant attachment. It's time to approach change from a place of self-compassion and nurturance.

Approaching change from a place of self-awareness and self-acceptance is a hallmark of secure attachment. For effective change, you must first recognize that your value and worth is constant and inherent. Your worth is not at all dependent on making changes. You deserve to make changes based on your needs, desires, and what would feel most supportive of the life you want.

When you dismantle the internalized cultural messaging that's taking you further from yourself, you can put your reclaimed energy into building awareness, connection, and trust with yourself. This foundational work will support you in making changes that bring you closer to the feelings you want and the life you truly desire. To do that, it's important to look at change from a different perspective. Remember, we're done trying HARDER.

Here are the ideas, theories, models, and practices for change that helped me and my clients the most. If you already have an understanding of the change process or practices that work for you, use them, and see how they can be layered with those below.

Phases of Trauma Healing

When I learned of the Phases of Trauma Healing, developed by Judith Herman, it deepened my understanding that healing work in your relationship with food and your body, especially of attachment wounds, is trauma healing. Healing requires a mix of emotional processing and having a new experience in the world. The Phases of Trauma Healing also highlight the importance of feeling safe and resourced before change can happen.

Yeah, but... I don't think I have trauma.

Do you feel like you're a failure, not good enough, or like there's something wrong with you? Do you have unhealed emotional wounds? Isn't that why you're here?

If you're deeply unsatisfied with your relationship with food and your body, there's a lot more going on below the surface than just disordered eating. It's an indicator that you have trauma. I like the definition of trauma given by Dr. Jaimie Marich: any unhealed wound.

Trauma isn't just what happened to you, but how your body responded to it. Trauma happens when experiences are too much, too soon, too fast, or too big for you at that moment. Trauma can also occur as the result of not getting enough of your basic needs met for too long. Trauma develops when you don't have the capacity or resources to deal with the size or intensity of an experience.

Often, it's the *lack of support* that makes the difference between a painful experience and lasting trauma. Trauma can be the result of being alone with a hurt and a lack of support in navigating the experience or the aftermath.

Beyond having clear traumatic experiences like neglect or abuse, as someone who's reading this book, you've likely developed trauma directly from diet culture and your caregivers' messages stemming from it.

Children will adopt a narrative that there's something wrong with them in order to keep the bond with their caregivers and community. This is internalization of diet culture messaging that there's something wrong with their body, its appearance, or the signals that come from their body like hunger, emotions, needs, and desires.

Maintaining the bond with caregivers is necessary for survival. When you're told there's something wrong with you, and you have to adopt this narrative to keep a bond with others, it causes an attachment rupture. It's effectively being forced to tell yourself, *yes, my caregivers are right, there's something wrong with me.* You were too young to be able to maintain your agency, know better, and stand up against these messages, so you self-abandoned. This creates a deep attachment wound, a rupture in your attachment to yourself. How can you trust yourself if you believe deeply that there's something inherently wrong with you? Doesn't that sound like trauma?

It's NOT your fault.

I'm here with you. It's time to heal. And it's important to take it one step at a time.

When you have an injury or wound, but are still in danger, your body will hold off on healing and perform only crisis management until you're safe. Once you're safe and your body can focus on healing, it has to first break down/metabolize the broken bones or inflammatory byproducts (like white blood cells) that rushed to the area before it can build you back up.

After healing, you test out the newly healed part of your body. You move through the world again and your body begins building new maps of being.

In healing emotional trauma, just like physical wound healing, your body must feel safe enough to prioritize healing: only then are you ready to metabolize (feel and process through) the grief of your traumatic experiences. Once you've processed through the grief, you can create new maps for experiences and move through the world differently.

Another way to think of this process is like remodeling a bathroom. First, you have to gather information, tools, and support. Next, it's demolition time! It might be hard to even imagine what it'll look like until you have a blank slate. Then, as you slowly put the bathroom back together, it begins to take shape. Years later, you might barely remember what the old bathroom was like.

Let's dive into each of the Phases of Trauma Healing as they apply to trauma and attachment wound healing. I created this graphic[19] by adapting Judith Herman's Phases of Trauma Healing because I find having a visual about where you're at in your healing process can be helpful. Keep in mind that life, healing, and change are not linear, and you might be in different phases of healing for different aspects of your relationship with yourself and your body. This is just a guide. Take what's helpful and leave the rest.

---

19. By "I created," I mean I explained the concept to my awesome VA (virtual assistant) who brought it to life. Thank you, Brooke! Investing in a VA is one of the ways I resource myself as a neurodivergent person to minimize barriers to getting stuff done… it's a privilege and has helped me be effective. When you can, get help!

Phases of Trauma Healing

Adapted from Judith Herman

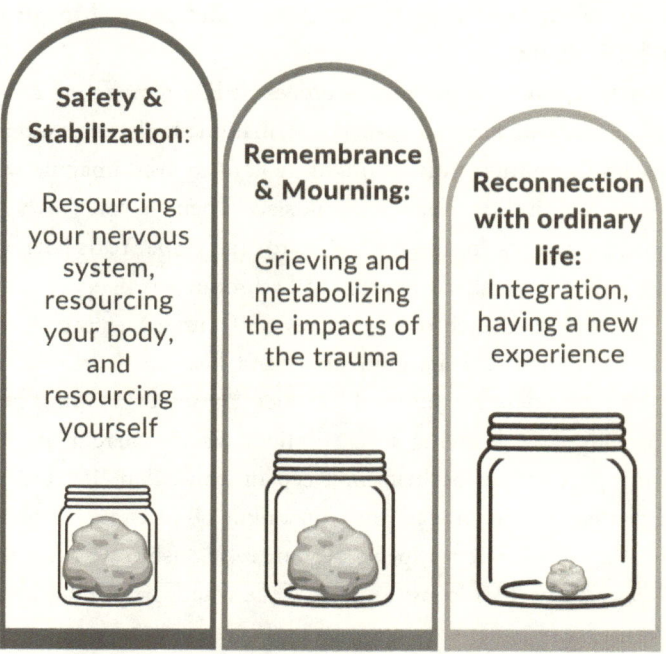

Safety & Stabilization:

Resourcing your nervous system, resourcing your body, and resourcing yourself

Remembrance & Mourning:

Grieving and metabolizing the impacts of the trauma

Reconnection with ordinary life:

Integration, having a new experience

Safety & Stabilization: Resourcing the Body

In this phase, you start out under-resourced, meaning you don't have all the support, tools, or skills you need to make the changes you want. At this stage, your nervous system is often dysregulated. Your jar is small… aka your capacity for life challenges and healing is low. The boulders in the graphic above represent unhealed wounds or trauma. You have big boulders that fill your jar, preventing you from healing and creating the changes you so desperately want.

Your trauma has kept you in survival mode. Often, I find that clients have been trying to change while they're vastly under-resourced and not feeling safe or supported. This can be one of the biggest reasons for feeling stuck. Before you try to dive into deeper healing work, or make big changes, you need to increase your capacity for healing.

Most of the people I talk to who are struggling with food are under-resourced. Some have food scarcity, some have financial insecurity, most have overburdened schedules, and almost all have a lack of really good emotional support.

The first phase of trauma healing is resourcing yourself, your nervous system, and your body. This can be really difficult in our capitalist society. Remember...

It's not your fault. You are not broken.

While being under-resourced is a barrier, it doesn't mean healing isn't possible. You may need to back up a bit and slow down. Give yourself some time to figure out what you need and where you already have resources you can lean on, then give yourself time to gather more resources, if needed. We'll do this work throughout the book. If you want to explore this more, I love the podcast *The Space Beyond Scarce* by Kate Holly for thinking differently about resources. She supports listeners to think deeply about values, needs, and desires—and how you might access them now.

Angel Austin of Sacred Space for Fat Bodies reminds us that sometimes survival is living in sustained trauma. This can be a result of an inability to leave the job, the abusive relationship, or the housing situation. Living amongst various systems of oppression can make it impossible to become safe, for example. If this is your experience, know that you shouldn't have been put in this position in the first place. I encourage you to give yourself all the compassion. Understand that your capacity may be limited for this work, and the opportunity will still be here when you're ready. Please take the parts that feel accessible; find softness here and wherever else you can. If surviving is what you're able to do, know that it means something. Steal moments of pleasure and space for yourself to be you. Living in a world that's making life feel impossible is an act of rebellion.

Remembrance and Mourning: Metabolizing Your Grief, Trauma, and Wounds

In the previous phase, you increased the size of your jar. Your capacity for deeper work expanded. The size of your trauma is still just as big, but you'll have a bit more breathing room as it no longer takes up all of your capacity. You're more resourced and feel safe to dive into the pain of your unhealed trauma.

I find folks naturally move into this stage, metabolizing their trauma, when resourced enough. Feelings organically start to bubble up. It can be confusing because it often feels hard, painful, or scary to finally process these experiences. That doesn't mean you aren't making progress. It's a sign that you *are*. You may feel discombobulated in this phase, so remember, *you're processing grief.* While grieving, things often don't feel like they make sense.

I recommend getting professional help with somatic work from a therapist or trained coach. Somatic work (feeling the sensations of the body and allowing them to guide your discovery) can help you process trauma in a safe space, guided by someone you trust.

To metabolize something is to use it up or utilize the valuable components and break down the rest into waste that can be excreted. Similarly, emotional metabolization is to fully experience the emotion and the parts that make it up, so it's no longer built up or stuck in your body. There are parts of your experiences that are important to hold onto, parts to simply feel, and parts to let go.

Metabolizing your unhealed pain can be done in many ways, just as grief is unique in each culture and for each person. Somatic work has been extremely helpful for me and my clients. Some practices that can be helpful are shaking, crying, art, body work, therapy such as Emotional Transformation Therapy or safe EMDR, and movement modalities such as martial arts and dancing. In Chapter 6, I provide a helpful somatic practice.

Reconnection with Ordinary Life: Integration
After metabolizing many of the emotions around your traumatic experiences, you may feel as though you've come undone. This process is an identity crisis of sorts. It requires reorienting to the world and to yourself in a new and unfamiliar way. It's like trying to remember how to walk after healing a broken leg. You'll never be quite the same. You still have the old experiences of walking around in the world, using stairs, etc., but your body is different. You're finding a new way of moving through life; a new way of being. You're creating new body maps.

Fortunately, in this phase, you have an even larger jar, you're even more resourced, and you've done so much healing work. Your trauma will always be there to some degree. After all, you *did* experience it, and that will never change, but it takes up so much less space now. Your trauma no longer rules your life, keeping you stuck in survival mode. You can move through the world differently and have new experiences.

Where do you feel you are currently in your healing journey? Do you need to stabilize and create more safety? Access more resources? Support your nervous system? Are you grieving, processing, or metabolizing through the trauma? Are you learning how to move through the world as you are now, after all that healing work?

> *Wherever you are, you're in the right place;*
> *it's all part of the change process.*

The Phases of Trauma Healing can be beautifully layered with other change models and practices. Let's check out another model that I feel is valuable and complimentary. I love the way this next one expands on the phases and speaks to the flow of change.

Safety and Softening First

This is a change model I learned from Dr. Satya Sardonicus, DC, creator of the NeuroFascial Flow® Method. She created it in reference to the body, to healing injury. I believe it applies very eloquently to emotional healing, growth, and change as well. Though presented linearly, keep in mind: it isn't linear. You'll likely go through the process many times or be in different phases about different parts of your growth at any given time, so use this primarily as a guide to understanding your process.

Here are the phases:
- establishing safety
- softening
- expansion
- re-establishing safety
- integration

Establishing Safety

If you don't feel safe, you can't prioritize growth, healing, or change. Feeling unsafe tells your nervous system that it must prioritize survival. A past mentor, Kevin Moore of the Reembody Method®, teaches that under threat, you'll return to the behavior patterns and strategies you developed as an infant, child, and young adult—because they worked. You survived, but didn't necessarily thrive. Your nervous system bases decisions on past experiences. This makes sense from a survival standpoint, but makes it hard to create sustainable change if you feel unsafe and revert to old patterns much of the time.

Just how does one establish safety? First, it's important to remember that for many people, the world isn't safe. We have to acknowledge systemic oppression, here. Feeling safe in your skin is exponentially more difficult in a world that tells you that there's something inherently wrong with you (or is even violent toward you) based on the color of your skin, your body size or shape (especially if superfat+), your sexual orientation, your gender, etc. Naming these systems, and accounting for them when you're thinking about what safety looks like for you, can be helpful. It's also VERY difficult to feel safe if you don't have enough resources to get your basic needs met. In *Burnout*, Emily Nagoski and Amelia Nagoski discuss the power of reminding yourself that the game is rigged.

These inequities are deeply harmful to your safety. This work is written from the lens of whiteness and other privileges, making it less than ideal for discussion around safety, but I want you to know that I see you, and I understand that it's frustrating to have to adapt yet another book to your needs. See Chapter 10 for more about this and the concept of whiteness as a barrier to secure attachment.

These tools will always be here. And it can be powerful to recognize that you need more resourcing for them to be accessible. It's perfectly okay if you decide to shift gears and focus on building more internal and external safety, resources, or stability instead of focusing on your relationship with food and your body... but I'd encourage you to keep reading because learning how to insulate yourself against diet culture can help you feel safer in your body. And your body is your forever home.

"If you can't be at home in your body, where are you supposed to go?"
— **Marilyn Wann,** *FAT!SO?*

It's important to remember safety doesn't equal comfort. Change is often uncomfortable. Confronting your own internalized anti-fat bias will likely be deeply uncomfortable but vital in helping you to feel safe in your body. Confronting those internalized messages will enable you to STOP beating yourself up. When you no longer constantly beat yourself up, your nervous system can exhale.

How to establish safety is something that each person must discover for themselves. What I need to feel safe is different than what you need to feel safe. It's an ongoing process, so you'll need to assess and re-assess as you move through life and this healing process.

To start, consider these reflection questions.

- What types of support feel good to you?
- What situations do you feel more open in?
- What situations allow you to be playful or to learn new things?
- What makes you feel closed?
- Who in your life makes you feel seen, heard, understood, or appreciated?
- Who in your life makes you shut down or hide who you really are?
- Where can you be yourself?
- What communities help you feel supported?
- What actions help you feel better when you're anxious?[20]

---

20. It's perfectly okay if food is one way you feel safe. I will NOT take that away from you. But I do encourage you to find additional ways to feel safe.

Softening

When you feel safe, your body can soften, and as you soften, you'll be more open and able to see things from different or new perspectives. Softening speaks to allowing yourself and your body *time*. Our culture encourages doing everything right now, but that doesn't give the body time to warm up. You know the feeling when you first lie down after a stressful day? It almost hurts as the stiffness leaves your body. After a bit, your body relaxes enough that you can stretch and settle. This is such an important but overlooked in-between stage—between wanting to feel different and actively moving toward it. Give your body time to prepare.

Softening is best facilitated if you're intentional about connecting to and supporting your body and nervous system.

Here are some ways you might consider supporting yourself in softening:

- breathing[21,22]
- giving yourself ample time or moving slowly
- touch
- tuning in to your body sensations
- yoga, dance, or other gentle movement practices
- singing
- verbal processing with someone you trust
- positive self-talk
- somatic coaching or therapy

---

21. My whole life people told me to breathe. I was like, "Clearly, I'm breathing. I'm alive, right?" Then I learned a technique called "oxy breathing" by Ellie Drake. It refers to the oxytocin that's released by expanding your diaphragm and stimulating your vagus nerve. It felt amazing and I began to embrace taking the time to deeply exhale and take expansive breaths as a regular, intentional, softening practice.

22. If people telling you to breathe makes you bristle, just ignore this. There's a reason people say that but... it's not helpful if it just pisses you off.

- community spaces that help you feel connected to your body
- being in nature
- soaking in warm water

What are the ways that you soften that come naturally to you or practices you already have in place? What would you like to try in the future? Please don't "should" yourself; the goal is to expand your options for softening, not to feel bad about something you think you "should" do.

Expansion

Expansion is where the magic happens—stretching the limits of what you've perceived is possible, especially if something has felt impossible or inaccessible. During this phase, you're literally creating new wiring. It can feel like a breakthrough moment where your perspective shifts, and you begin to see a path to the change you'd like to have.

In expansion, you explore what your barriers or unhealed wounds are really about. This involves processing through emotions and gaining clarity about your underlying needs, wants, or desires. From there, you begin to see how to support yourself in moving forward.

At times, this internal shift is instantaneous. Other times, it takes repeated attempts at it, as change often requires small shifts over time. Some of us want to live here, constantly expanding... but that isn't how bodies or change works. It's not expansion if you're constantly stretched to your limit.

In my experience, expansion happens naturally when we feel safe, supported, and resourced, and when we consistently show up for ourselves and our growth work. Many change models speak to readiness. Readiness considers your desire to change but also your bandwidth or capacity. Attempting to force change only results in feeling shame when we aren't able to make the shifts we hoped for.

Some questions to reflect on:

- What's my capacity for change right now?
- How well do I feel supported right now?
- Do I have support that feels right for this desired change?
- In what ways do I feel resourced?
- In what ways do I feel I could be better resourced to approach the changes I'd like to make?
- Am I consistently showing up for growth work? If not, what would help me be more consistent?

Another shameless plug for somatic coaching with an anti-diet provider here. Having a consistent, safe space to process your challenges around your relationship with food and your body is so helpful. In my experience, somatic work is highly effective in supporting folks in experiencing expansive growth around food and body relationships. There are many other ways as well, but this is my personal favorite. Each person is unique, so exploring what feels right for you is so important. If you can't access coaching or therapy, consider finding online or in-person support groups and commit to participating regularly.

Re-establishing Safety

Expansion can feel amazing but it's often taxing for your brain and body. After expansion, your body needs to have a period of rest and time to reorient in the world. Your body needs to know that even though you've made a (scary) change, you're okay.

You might find yourself feeling low energy, cocooning or soothing via TV, eating, shopping, scrolling, or [insert comforting behavior here]. You might feel like you're taking two steps back after making progress. It can catch you off guard if you're expecting to power through or never go back to old patterns. Remember that those patterns are there for a reason, helping you feel safe.

Give yourself as much compassion and non-judgment as possible during this phase. Rather than judgment and self-shaming, what you need and deserve during this process is support.

Integration

Integration is where, in your day-to-day life, you practice what you've learned during expansion. This is when behavioral changes deepen and become habits. You begin to experience a new way of being. Integration requires testing your new awareness and skills in different environments or situations, strengthening and expanding upon wiring created during the expansion phase.

I find that many people expect change to just be like the flip of a switch, and you do things differently forevermore. It can happen like that, but it usually doesn't. More often, you need to practice these behavioral changes in small ways before approaching more challenging situations. If something feels big, like setting a boundary with your parents, try practicing with your coach or therapist, rehearsing in the mirror, or setting boundaries with others you feel safer with first so you can build some experience.

Remember to celebrate every one of your small steps at each stage. They add up!

Aligned Change

I used to approach change from an outside-in or top-down perspective. I'd take a "should" and attempt to impose it on my body. I'd try to fight against my nature, thinking there was something wrong with the way I was naturally. This made change extremely difficult, if not impossible, and furthered my feelings of shame and a lack of self-trust. It was so painful.

I tried so many hacks, spreadsheets, and accountability programs, thinking that this time, I'd get my shit together, only to end up thinking I was weak because I couldn't maintain the changes.

Now, rather than relying on an external "should" or an internalized narrative about how I want my body to behave, I turn to my body to guide me in making choices about how I want to be and what I want to experience. I also check in with my body about its needs and bandwidth for change. In addition to setting goals and striving to make changes that are affirming to my whole self, rather than those originating from shame, I've shifted the way I approach change.

Rather than restricting, controlling, or contorting myself to fit into someone else's ideas of how I "should" be, I consult my body. Then I add in what's needed. Additive goals are so much more powerful than trying to take something away. For example, setting a goal to eat one serving of veggies per day instead of restricting sweets.

Now I also use strength-based goals (aka using strategies you've already had success with or techniques that rely on your inherent strengths). I've stopped fighting myself, and instead, go with my natural rhythms and ways of being. After all, there's nothing wrong with the way I am—neurodivergence, disabilities, and all! This approach is not only wayyyy more effective, but it also creates a more nurturing relationship with your*self.*

The next chapter is all about body attunement, somatic practices, and practical tools to build connection and trust with your*self* and to become an intuitive eater. Take what works for you and leave the rest. Do this work one step at a time as your capacity allows.

> *My body is my home, my ally,*
> *not my enemy.*

Chapter Six

Body Attunement

Developing the skill of body attunement (becoming aware of [or tuned in to], trusting, and responding to your body's signals) is key to intuitive eating and to coming to a place of earned secure attachment with your*self*, your body, and food. Unfortunately, body attunement isn't prioritized in Western and other cultures, or in many families, so you now have the task of building this skill. One barrier to body attunement is receiving the message that you can't trust yourself, or that it isn't safe to prioritize your body's needs—which disproportionately affects people with marginalized identities, especially those with multiple intersecting marginalized identities.

Most people won't have this skill of body attunement developed yet when they pick up this book. There's a difference between not having the skill developed and having the inability to develop the skill. Sometimes an inability to develop this skill is temporary—due to barriers that need to be addressed—or permanent due to physiology such as alexithymia (the inability to feel bodily sensations). If you try these practices and they aren't working for you, please don't judge yourself. You may need a different approach or more support. There's more information on barriers to body attunement and secure attachment in Chapter 10.

A note about disability and pain: disability can be a barrier that's both temporary and permanent. The impact of your disabilities may fluctuate from day to day, making it hard to have the bandwidth to practice these skills. Pain can make tuning in to your body feel scary, very hard, or even impossible. Dissociation is a survival tool when your body needs to shut down due to pain or lack of capacity. Please don't judge yourself for it, but do gently assess if you can be open to new experiences. Practice these skills on the days they feel accessible. As you practice them, you'll likely find that connecting with your body feels less uncomfortable and yields more benefits. You'll be better equipped to care for yourself as you are each day.

Many barriers to body attunement and secure attachment involve the development of brain wiring over time. You may have pre-existing wiring that tells you that you aren't safe, aren't good enough, and need to act in a certain way to survive. This is true of addiction, pain, people-pleasing, disordered eating patterns, and more. The great thing about practicing body attunement is that it literally creates new wiring. Wiring that supports connection and trust with yourself. Let's begin re-wiring!

The first step to developing body attunement is awareness. When you want to change something, you have to first become aware of automatic thoughts that keep you stuck. Martin M. Broadwell is credited for creating a model known as "the four levels of teaching." The levels are unconscious incompetence, conscious incompetence, conscious competence, and unconscious competence. I don't love the use of the word "incompetence" due to the negative associations we collectively have, but this model is helpful for illustrative purposes.

Before change can happen or a new habit can be developed, you aren't conscious of your lack of skill. Through reading this book, you're becoming more aware of some of the barriers to having the kind of relationship with food and your body that you really want.

You're likely now in the conscious incompetence stage: aware of your lack of skill in this area, but unable to do it differently. That awareness can be painful, but it's an important step toward becoming competent in the skills, habits, and tools you need to make the changes you want.

Next, you become competent through practice, but you have to consciously put in effort to use your new skills and will often slip back into old patterns. This is when you're likely to have that "one step forward, two steps back" frustration.

In the last phase, these new skills become auto-pilot. You don't even have to think about them anymore. You develop a new habit, and it becomes muscle memory.

I share this model here to illustrate the importance of the first step, bringing awareness to the unconscious thoughts, patterns, beliefs, and behaviors standing in your way of secure attachment with food and yourself. I also hope it'll help you understand that progress isn't as simple as wanting to change and doing it. It isn't typically comfortable either. Like a child learning to ride a bike, you'll have to experience the pain of not being competent at something and having a few falls along the way.[23]

Knowing is different from understanding and practicing. Bringing awareness to your thoughts is an important first step. Going a step beyond by experiencing your bodily sensations—and exploring the unhealed wounds that give rise to your thoughts—is so much more effective.

Let's look at some tools that will help you build body attunement. As we dive in, keep in mind that you may experience noise that can make these practices more challenging, such as negative self-talk, feeling a block, or shutting down when you try to tune in to your body. This noise is the result of feeling unsafe, outside

---

23. I literally ran into a mailbox and a giant cedar tree while learning to ride my bike. Thanks, Dad! You said you'd hold on!

conditioning, and internalizing messages that you can't trust yourself. For example, people in larger bodies have often had to disconnect from their bodies to survive societal harassment. Remind yourself that these are past survival strategies, go slow, and work on creating safety for yourself as you practice the new tools.

The 5A's Tool

This is my go-to way of helping clients build understanding, connection, and trust with their body. The 5A's are:

- awareness
- acceptance
- allowing
- acknowledgment
- action? (honoring)

I created the 5A's tool to support clients in creating the space and structure to fully process their emotions and sensations. The 5A's involves connecting to your body's experience, following your body's lead, and showing appreciation for your body's guidance.

So often, people either ignore their body's signals or try to change them without spending time *understanding* and *experiencing* them fully first. As you read through the 5A's, keep in mind the first 4A's are the most important—simply put, deeply feeling and accepting what your body is expressing with kindness and curiosity rather than trying to control, manage, push, or ignore it.

Awareness
**Bring awareness to the sensations that
are happening in your body.**

Awareness may sound simple, but becoming aware of what's happening internally is challenging for most people. It's especially hard when you've spent much of your life in survival mode. Awareness can be a powerful antidote to not feeling seen after a lifetime of being told to disregard your body's signals, needs, and desires.

Focus on awareness of the sensations you're feeling first. Choose one area or sensation to zero in on. Ideally, you'll focus more on your visceral sensations, such as throat, chest, and abdomen areas, rather than musculoskeletal sensations, such as shoulder tightness. Try to avoid good/bad judgments and simply observe what's there (if you're having difficulty with this step, work on the next two steps, acceptance and allowing, and come back to this one).

Here are some helpful reflection questions to make this experience a bit more concrete: is the sensation pleasant or unpleasant? Does it have a color? Texture? A movement or direction? A temperature? Do your best to describe its qualities. At this stage, use sensation words like "buzzing" or "vibrating" rather than feelings like "anxiety" or "sadness."

If you find yourself coming up with a feeling word, it can be helpful to ask yourself, "How do I know I feel X emotion? What's that sensation like in my body? Where do I feel X emotion in my body?"

Acceptance

Acceptance of whatever sensations and emotions you're experiencing. You aren't bad or wrong for feeling this way.

You may struggle with acceptance after years of being told that you should ignore your body's signals, or from simply being in a survival state. That makes complete sense.

Having acceptance for whatever you're feeling is so important. Very often, I see clients pushing away their feelings or disconnecting or disassociating from their body because they don't think their feelings are safe or acceptable. For example, Black women might avoid feeling or expressing anger in an attempt to avoid being put into a harmful racial stereotype. But all people deserve to feel the full spectrum of feelings. Cutting off acceptance of yourself adds to dehumanization and creates a hostile internal environment. It also might lead to those feelings coming out in ways you'd rather they didn't. Accepting that it's valid to feel whatever you're feeling creates connection and internal safety.

You may want to say something like, "All of this is valid. There's room for all of this here. It's okay to feel this way. Whatever I'm feeling makes sense."

YOU ARE NOT BROKEN

If you find that it's difficult to accept whatever is coming up, try spending some time with the part of you that is afraid or resistant. The resistant part of you is also valid and important to understand. If you're struggling, it can be helpful to see a somatic practitioner or therapist—one who does Internal Family Systems or Parts work can be especially helpful with this.

Allowing

Allow sensations (and associated emotions) within your body to take up space, be seen, and felt. This phase is when you *feel* your feelings and metabolize/process them.

I like to think of allowing as giving that part of me the stage for a bit, or simply as experiencing the sensation more fully. For many people, actually experiencing sensations in their body can be overwhelming. Sensations can feel so big, especially when you've been pushing them away for so long. Start small: spend four or five breaths or 20 seconds feeling a sensation. Play with the volume level (intensity) of the sensation—you can turn it up or down. After practicing this for a bit, you can work your way up to more time at a higher intensity. Most feelings are like a wave that'll lessen in intensity after a short time—around 60-90 seconds. While allowing, you may get information from that part. It might be simply the sensation; it could be an association, images, memories, or thoughts. Just take note and stay curious.

It can also be helpful to spend time feeling more pleasant sensations as well. Allowing sensations to take up space is a skill that grows any time you practice it. Try it whenever you notice something fun or pleasant. For example, when you notice the way your belly tingles after going over a big hill in your car, allow that sensation to grow for a bit. If you notice a warmth spreading throughout your body when you get a hug from someone you care about, practice allowing that sensation as well! It all counts, and it all builds connection.

For some, especially fat people, pleasure hasn't been allowed. It may take time to feel safe allowing yourself to feel pleasure. As adrienne maree brown shows us in *Pleasure Activism*, it can be one of the most incredible acts of rebellion.

I find that most people skip the allowing stage when trying to process emotions or past trauma. You can't metabolize something by thinking about it. You have to actually feel it to work through it. But again, be gentle. If this is feeling too hard, look for ways you can resource yourself and create more safety around experiencing the sensations in your body. You can also do practices that support moving the feeling through, such as throwing ice cubes or kicking pinecones, shredding paper, dancing, stomping, singing loudly, yelling, progressive muscle squeezes, or scribbling. A somatic therapist or coach can be so supportive for metabolizing feelings.

Acknowledgment
**Acknowledge the information your body
gave you with appreciation.**

Acknowledgment is supportive in building the relationship with your body. There are two aspects of acknowledgment: naming your experiences and expressing appreciation.

First, put words to your experiences. You might name the color, textures, or imagery you noticed as you allowed your sensations full expression. You might also name the emotions associated with the sensations you felt. This helps your executive brain engage, which will support long-term skill building, and help you figure out what you need.

Then, acknowledge that part of you or the sensation for helping you know yourself better. Expressing appreciation for the experience of feeling your body sensations tells your nervous system that it's safe and good to listen to your body.

Next, acknowledge and appreciate your body for all it does, all it carries, and the way it signals your needs. This is a way to reinforce that your body signaling you is a GOOD thing—something you want your body to keep doing. It's also a way to practice gratitude toward your body, your home, after years of bullying and negative self-talk toward it.

I like to say, "Thank you, body, for getting my attention, for creating these sensations to guide me, for carrying me through life, and for bringing me to who I am in this moment in time."

Use the words that make sense to you. If words don't feel authentic yet, you can simply feel the energy of appreciation and try sending it to the part of yourself you were getting to know better. It may feel awkward at first but stick with it.

Next, it's time to shift from your internal experience back into the world around you. I like to give my body gentle squeezes, like a hug, and stretch while looking around my room. This is another way I convey my appreciation to my body. More about this practice in the final section of this chapter.

Acknowledgment and appreciation for your body might be difficult if you feel your body has failed you, especially for disabled folks. Please give yourself space to feel any grief that comes up. The 5A's is a practice that shows your body that you value its messages and care for it, regardless of how it performs from day to day. You and your body deserve this respect, care, and attention.

Action? (Honoring)
Honor the information you learned from your body in the first four A's.

Time to take action! Right? Maybe, *maybe not*. The goal of body attunement isn't to fix or change your feelings. It's more about honoring the information you received by checking in with your body. Sometimes the action is simply having checked in with your body, acknowledging the sensations, feelings, and experiences present for you.

Or maybe there is an action needed to honor the info you received. This is usually an unmet need. Maybe it's that there's a boundary that needs to be set. Or maybe you need to metabolize some grief. There's no right way or timeline, but figuring out how to get those needs met is important. You might need to set aside alone time, schedule an appointment with your therapist, do some journaling, or find other ways to get more clarity. You might also need to resource yourself before taking action.

Being securely attached, in a nurturing relationship with yourself and your body, means looking at yourself holistically. When trying to get a need met or make a change, it requires honoring your bandwidth for taking action. It can help to ask yourself, "What's my capacity right now?" and "How resourced and ready am I to take action on this?" If a boundary needs to be set with someone, but you aren't really prepared to have that conversation, you aren't really resourced for it, or it's not the best time for you, it's important to acknowledge that. You might tell yourself, "Yes, this needs to happen at some point, but I'm also not quite ready." Consider what you need to move toward honoring the underlying need.

Whatever you learn about yourself and your needs, the goal is to be in relationship with it. This means not just automatically taking an action, but instead spending that time reflecting on what would feel the most supportive and nurturing in this moment, and going forward.

Landing

How often do you pause in your day between activities? Giving yourself a moment to see how you're feeling? We tend to rush between things all day long, never giving our body's signals a moment on the stage. Taking a few minutes to land is especially helpful during transitions in your day so that you can process what is coming up in real time, be present for the next thing, and avoid a big build-up of stress as your day barrels on.

Here's a simple landing exercise I developed that incorporates the 5A's (it takes about 10 minutes). It helps with building body attunement, nurturing your connection with yourself, and learning how to honor your body's signals. Think of this as checking your internal weather or doing a pulse check. Ideally, you'll practice this grounding exercise or a condensed version of it a few times a day—during transitions like between work and your evening time, after the kids go to bed, while walking the dog, as you begin to relax for the evening, or before or after experiences that cause you stress.

If you'd like to hear me guide you through it rather than read it, go to the Resources section at the end of the book for an audio option.[24]

Take a few deep exhales. Begin noticing, what does the support under you feel like? How do you know that it's supportive? What does that support feel like against your body? What's your relationship to that support? Are you able to relax into it a little more?

Shift your attention and notice what the surfaces of the rest of your body feel like. How does the air feel against your skin? What does gravity feel like against your body? Can you allow gravity to bring you a little closer to the earth? Can you lean more heavily on the support under you? How does it feel to be held?

Turn your attention inward. What does it feel like inside your body? Do an energy check—as if you're checking the weather. Ask yourself, "What sensations am I feeling?"

Give yourself some acceptance. Tell yourself, "Whatever I'm feeling makes sense. It's valid. There's room for all of this here." No judgment here; stay curious whether you feel connected or disconnected, whether it's quiet internally or loud. There's no right way to be, only what's currently present for you.

Now choose one area, one part of you, or one sensation to zero in on. Ideally, this is something in your visceral area (the area of

---

24. A client once told me this exercise is better than Xanax!

your body where your soft organs are, so anywhere from your groin to your mouth). Just simply notice what's present, being close to that part of you. The only goal is getting to know yourself and that part of you a little bit better.

Do your best to describe the sensations that are present. Be careful to not name emotions (yet) or what you think is making you feel this way (that's a narrative about what you're feeling). Simply feel and describe the sensation. What's the temperature? Are you feeling heat or coolness? Is this area relaxed or tight? Perhaps you're feeling spaciousness. Maybe it's cavernous in there. Maybe you're feeling a buzzing or tingling electricity. Does this part of you have a movement or a direction to it? Does it have a color or texture? Simply observe whatever is present for you in this moment with curiosity and compassion. The goal is to get know this part of you better.

Allow this part of you to take up as much space as it would like, to be as loud or intense as it needs to be. For just a few moments, allow the sensation to have the stage. You might invite it to grow in size and intensity.

Get curious: does this part have any information for you, anything it'd like you to know, or anything it'd like to feel or experience from you in this moment?

Now provide this part with some support or nurturance. What would feel supportive may be clear, and if not, experiment. Perhaps it's just nurturance and compassion—try giving that part of you a metaphorical hug. Maybe it's some reassurance, permission, or forgiveness. It might be an action or acknowledgment that something needs to happen. A boundary might need to be set, you might need to carve out more rest time, or you might need some space for grieving. See if you can give this part a bit of that support or nurturance right now, in this moment. Notice if what you're offering feels right. Then notice if you're able to receive that nurturance from yourself or not. Again, with no judgment, as there's no right or wrong here. We're simply trying to get to know ourselves better and learn what your body and different parts of you need to feel seen and supported.

Zooming out a little bit, see if there are any other needs being signaled by your body that perhaps you can't attend to in this moment. It can be a physical need or an emotional one. Perhaps you need to go to the restroom. Maybe you're thirsty or need some rest. Or maybe there's deeper work to be done—other parts of you that need attention and time on the stage. Give yourself some reassurance that you're paying attention and will take care of these needs. In your own words, say to yourself, "I hear you. I'm listening. These feelings, needs, and desires are valid. I'll return to attend to you as I'm able."

Provide some acknowledgment and appreciation for your body. Give yourself some love. It might be helpful to put your hand on your heart or your belly. Say in your own words some form of gratitude. "Thank you, body. Thank you for getting my attention. Thank you for carrying me and holding all of my internal experience. Thank you for all that you do to keep things running as I move about the world. Thank you for bringing me to who I am in this moment in time."

Now, focus on the outside edges of your body, giving yourself gentle squeezes or stretches to help reintegrate back into the world around you. Touch the parts of your body that are accessible. Stretching or squeezing will wake up your body's proprioceptors (the signals that tell your brain where your body is in space). Next, open your eyes and look around. This helps expand your peripheral vision. These actions give your body more information about how your body feels and what the environment is like. They help regulate your nervous system and remind your body that you're safe. Take a few more deep exhales as you reorient to your environment.

Touching Your Body

You may have noticed that I mentioned giving yourself gentle squeezes at the end of the landing exercise. Am I suggesting you hug yourself? Lol, yes. Yes, I am.

Giving yourself gentle touch helps build a loving, compassionate relationship with your body. It also helps with nervous system regulation by sending your body the message that you're safe and boosts feel-good hormones. And perhaps the biggest benefit: it helps reinforce, through physical action, that your body IS good, and it deserves to be treated well and cared for, regardless of how it looks or what it can do. How would you comfort a crying baby? Holding a baby is one of the best ways to show it that you care and that it's safe. You deserve that too… especially if you haven't received as much touch as you need or want, now or in the past.

Years ago, I began doing self-massage of my feet and worked my way up my body from there. At first it was activating because I saw my body as gross, bad, and wrong, whereas giving it gentle touch was a loving action. I had to work through the feeling that my body wasn't good enough to deserve love. Please note: I use the term "activating" in place of "triggering" for many reasons, but mainly because it's not ideal to avoid something just because it causes a nervous system response (activation). It's helpful to notice what's coming up, get curious about it, and then see what support you need.

After practicing touching myself regularly, I began to see my body as a human body that not only needed touch but also deserved it. If you find self-touch to be very activating, you may need to hold off on this and get support working through body shame first.

It can also be helpful to frame self-touch in other ways, such as putting on lotion as an enjoyable sensory experience, rather than as a self-care task. If you can't reach parts of your body that you'd like to, try modifying. Consider using blankets to wrap yourself with, or tools meant for self-massage to reach the parts of your body that are hard to access. This practice is meant to be supportive and connecting. Use it in whatever ways feel helpful.

My body is my home, my ally, not my enemy.

Useful Tools for Relating to Food Differently

Hunger

Honoring your hunger signals might sound like the simplest of Intuitive Eating's principles. And yet… it can be so complicated. For many folks who have been disconnected from their body or attempting to repress hunger signals, honoring hunger can feel impossible.

When I ask a new client if they're eating enough, they almost always say that they're not only eating enough, but too much! And diet culture has taught us to be terrified of eating too much. But when we look at what they've eaten in a day, it's usually not enough. At least, not enough during the day. Typically, they skip breakfast and just have coffee, eat only a quick snack for lunch, then are so hungry at night that they eat beyond fullness, or eat most of the evening and call it a binge. This is the body's savvy way of making up for a lack of food during the day: by increasing your drive to eat and diminishing fullness signals, aka primal hunger.

When I ask clients what hunger feels like in their body, if they're able to describe it at all, they most often describe primal hunger. When you ignore your body's hunger signals long enough, your body is forced to be really loud to make you pay attention. However, if you're very disconnected from your body or ignore the signals enough over time, your body might stop bothering with sending the signals altogether. This can also be complicated by weight loss surgeries or medications that suppress your hunger signals.

Start paying attention to what happens when you haven't eaten for 3-5 hours. If you don't feel anything other than low energy, you may need to go beyond simple awareness, as your body might need support in waking up or allowing hunger signals. You also might not have traditional hunger signals, as is more common for neurodivergent folks. If so, you may need to shift your focus on ways to remember to eat regularly that don't rely on hunger signals.

If you have any barriers to feeling hunger signals, you'll benefit from professional support by someone with specialized training around your specific challenges, and it might mean deciding to eat meals even when you aren't feeling hunger to support your body while you work on it.

Fullness

People are often much more concerned when they eat beyond fullness than they are about honoring hunger. This is due to shame and diet culture messaging that there's something wrong with you if you can't "control yourself." There's a reason that Intuitive Eating's principle of honoring your hunger comes first; you won't be able to recognize and honor fullness if you aren't eating when you're hungry, or if you aren't getting enough food.

It's helpful to shift from fixating on fullness to making satiety your goal. Fullness is often finicky. It relies on signals from your body that may or may not turn on due to many complex factors. This can also be complicated by past weight loss, gastrointestinal surgeries, or medications, which can cause premature fullness or diminish fullness signals.

There are day-to-day changes or environmental factors that can impact fullness. Are you bloated? You might feel full sooner. Did you eat while very distracted? You might feel full but not at all satisfied. Did you start out overly hungry? Most likely, you won't feel full until you've eaten way beyond fullness. Are you eating something that doesn't really taste good? You might feel full but not satisfied and crave something more. Have you ever asked a child if they're full and they say they are, but only full of dinner? They still have room for dessert. They're full but not satisfied. Or they aren't full but don't want more of the food they're eating, so they use claiming fullness to get out of eating. I stopped asking people I'm feeding if they're full, if they're done, or if they want more. Instead, I ask if they're satisfied. I extend this to myself as well.

Honoring hunger will create more ease around feeling fullness and satiety. This is one of the many reasons body attunement and the 5A's are so important and powerful. The first step is to become aware of what your hunger signals are, especially the more subtle signals. Then, work on accepting, allowing, appreciating, and honoring your hunger. This process builds trust with your body.

Here's a graphic to help discover your hunger and satiety sensations.

Hunger Sensations

What does hunger feel like?

Empty stomach
Thinking about food
Salivating
Emptiness/spaciousness in belly
Jaw tightness
Rumbling tummy
Burning in esophagus
Fogginess

What does satiety feel like?
(Do I feel satisified?)

Feeling of completeness
Filled to capacity
Feeling stuck to your ribs
Warmth
Pressure in the abdomen
Tightness in belly
Sluggish/sleepy
Heaviness

Come back when you're hungry (or about four hours from the last time you ate) and see what sensations you feel in your body. Then eat a meal you enjoy and come back to the list to see which fullness or satiety sensations you notice.

It can also be helpful to dive a bit deeper and understand degrees of hunger and fullness. Here's a hunger/fullness scale I created to help.[25]

How to Use the Hunger Scale

The goal of utilizing the hunger scale is to learn how to support your body around hunger and fullness. It can reveal patterns around hunger and fullness that aren't supporting your wellbeing, such as waiting too long to eat or eating to the point of discomfort. When using this tool, be careful to approach it with curiosity, not judgment.

I find this tool particularly useful for people who tend toward avoidance in their relationship with food, and for those who have divested thoroughly from diet culture and are ready to build body attunement. Please note that some people don't have the ability to feel hunger sensations due to neurodivergence, medical issues or surgery, and severe restriction. If this is you, don't judge yourself. Meet yourself where you're at and get support.

Ideally, you'd stay within the Happy Tummy Zone, but if you aren't connected to your hunger signals, you'll probably go from one extreme to another. Getting below level 3 hunger can be dangerous territory. You may experience being "hangry." You'll also be more likely to eat things that don't make you feel good. You will likely react to extreme hunger by eating quickly and past the point of fullness. Getting beyond a level 8 in fullness can cause discomfort, bloating, and indigestion. The physical discomfort and urgent

---

25. Thanks to the help of my was-band. If you're reading this, I really appreciated your support while I was starting to understand what I wanted to be when I grew up ☺

COACH TIFFANY'S
HUNGER SCALE

 **0** — I'm so hungry I could literally eat my arm. Why did I go so long without food? Actually upset. This is serious!

 **1** — HANGRY... Feed me or I'm going to lose my sh!t.

  2 — I'm sooo hungry. I want all the foodz! Just give me the whole box.

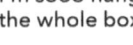

  3 — YES!! Time to eat. I love food!

  4 — I could wait a bit but I could definitely eat.

  5 — Half empty? Or half full?...Do I even have a stomach?

  6 — Not really hungry but could eat more!

  7 — Mmmm, that was good. I feel fullish, but I could probably fit in a few bites of dessert.

  8 — Wow! That was good. Now, where are my stretch pants?

Happy Tummy

 9 — Why, oh why, did I do this to myself???

  10 — I'm actually worried my stomach might burst open. I'm never eating again!

eating may cause negative self-talk and put you into a shame spiral. Please give yourself compassion if this happens.

If you find yourself regularly eating to level 9 or 10, or frequently let yourself get to level 2 or 1, it can be helpful to look at the surrounding circumstances—your stress level, overworking, putting others first, etc.—without judgment to see what's contributing to that pattern.

The hunger scale can also be used for self-care via planning ahead. It's helpful to pay attention to how long it takes you to get from level 5 to 4 or level 3 to 2 to help with planning meals in the future. If you know it only takes fifteen or twenty minutes for you to get from level 4 to 3 or from level 3 to 2, you'll want to seek out food when you're at level 4 or 5. If you're at level 4 and have two hours until dinner, you might want to eat a snack.

On the fullness end, it's helpful to know that if you eat to level 7 you may be hungry in about three hours, so if you're eating dinner at 5 p.m., eating to level 7 and then not planning to eat again before bed at 11 p.m., you might find you're too hungry at bedtime, for example. You may want to consider eating to level 8, having dinner later, or planning to eat a snack before bed.

The hunger scale is a guide to learn more about your body. Using it can be very helpful as long as it's employed with a lens of curiosity and without judgment. It isn't meant to be rigid or another diet. If you're anxious, preoccupied, or anxious avoidant, you might find that you have a tendency to beat yourself up if you eat beyond fullness. You might tend to try to use this scale perfectly or become overly focused on it. Remember, it's a guide. If it's too activating for you, you might not be ready for it, or it might not be right for you, and that's okay.

What to Eat

I almost wrote this entire book without talking about what to eat at all, lol. I was almost startled when it occurred to me that I hadn't included it in the outline. This is a clue about how little your relationship with food and your body revolves around what you eat. What and how you eat is a reflection of your experiences, preferences, access, and bandwidth. It isn't a good measure of success. But I know some of you appreciate more concrete guidance. Use this as a way to understand yourself better, not a measuring stick.

🍃 How do you relate to food?
🍃 How do you choose what, when why, where, and how to eat?

So much of the way most people relate to food is driven by unconscious beliefs that are just stealthy, internalized diet culture messages. Those messages create avoidance or preoccupation/anxiety which drive behaviors that aren't supportive to a satisfying relationship with food.

In the eating disorder treatment world, normative eating is often the focus... and so many clients say they want to eat "normally." The word "normal" implies there's a right way to eat, and that most people are doing it, so you should be able to as well. It can be so much more helpful to shift the focus to resonant eating.[26] Resonant eating speaks to meeting your unique needs and meeting yourself where you're at.

Bringing awareness to your unconscious beliefs, rejecting "shoulds," tuning in to your body, and using discernment are key to resonant eating. To sum it up as simply as I can: eat in a way that feels best for you, for who and where you are at this moment,

---

26. A term taught by the Embodied Recovery Institute: if you're a professional who treats people with eating disorders, I highly recommend their training.

considering future you as well, with the bandwidth you have in that moment. But if you want some additional guidance, here's some food for thought...

The 6W's Tool

Diet culture focuses almost entirely on WHAT and sometimes WHEN to eat (typically recommending restriction), but leaves out things like WHO (agency), WHY, WHERE, and HOW.

The 6W's are:

- who
- what
- when
- where
- why
- how

The 6W's can be a helpful framework for looking holistically at your relationship with food. Let's get curious and dive in!

Who?

YOU!! Only you get to decide what to eat. You might also consider guidance from your doctor—if they've done the work around their own internalized anti-fat bias or you have a medical condition like celiac disease that requires a very specific medically indicated diet. Be very careful here: doctors often prescribe a "medically indicated diet" for things like high cholesterol that aren't effective and are still just a restrictive diet dressed up as doctor-approved. In fact, anorexia, fasting, and starvation are associated with increased cholesterol (Northville, 2025). Sometimes the very things we're trying to treat with diets are made worse by them. I highly recommend, whenever possible, finding a doctor that practices from a Health at Every Size® lens and has done the work around their own internalized anti-fat bias.

You're the best person to determine what's best for you.

"Shoulds" don't work when it comes to eating. Embrace the power of personal choice.[27] Agency and autonomy are so important in your relationship with food and your body. Taking complete ownership over food choices can be really challenging if you don't trust yourself. Building body attunement will help with that. And it's a skill you're already building!

What is *best* doesn't mean the "healthiest" option. The litmus test I like to ask myself is:

> "*What would be the most nourishing and satisfying food for me, **given my capacity**?*"

At times, that might mean eating cookies because that's what sounds satisfying and is readily available. At times, that might mean having a salad for lunch because you need more fiber and it sounds tasty. There's no right answer.

If you've previously been under the influence of diet culture, you might've stopped eating food you crave, made certain foods off-limits, or had a rigid structure around eating. It's important to reject that restriction and rigidity. You'll likely need to let go of the rigid structure and intentionally eat an abundance of the previously restricted food. If your inner rebel is saying, *I'll eat what I want!*, that's valid. Get curious about what that rebellious part of you is saying, and what your underlying needs are. Claiming your autonomy around food and body choices can be extremely powerful.

However, just eating whatever over a long enough period is avoidance, and most likely won't feel great in the long term. This is where body attunement and discernment come into play. Where

---

27. My dear friend Natalie Forsythe, who's trained in Intuitive Eating and getting a degree in Social Work, taught me the importance of the power of choice in resonant eating. Thanks, friend!

you're at in your relationship with food and your body is a very important and valid factor. You won't stay in this stage forever if you're tuning in, assessing where you're at in your growth around food and body, and honoring your needs.

You're the only person who understands all your preferences and circumstances in your life that play into decisions around food choices. Only you know what resonates.

What?

Ideally, what to eat is guided by body attunement. Again, I can't stress this enough: it isn't helpful to try to follow a list of "shoulds." There's no right, correct, or best list of foods to eat. Each person is unique. For example, some people are extremely sensitive to caffeine and even a little bit makes their anxiety go through the roof. Others are impacted by it very little, and some are even helped by it, such as some folks with ADHD who find caffeine regulating.

Additive Goals

If you're newer to body attunement or are primarily eating foods that feel unsupportive of your body, it can be helpful to try eating well consistently. This is best accomplished by *adding* in nourishing food—remember, no restriction!

In addition to developing body attunement, here's a simple guideline: try to consistently eat meals that include carbs, fat, protein, and fiber. For most people, this is best for steadier blood sugar. Having steady blood sugar can help reduce crashes that leave you tired and struggling to regulate energy and mood.

To avoid restriction but still make some changes, focus on additive goals. One way to do this is to start with adding in a few more fruits and veggies per week. Most folks don't get enough fiber and adding in fruits and veggies is a great way to increase fiber intake. Please don't go out and drastically increase your fiber intake tomorrow—your gut will suffer from dramatic shifts. Fiber helps with regular bowel movements. Ideally, you eat consistently enough, are hydrated enough, and have regulated enough nervous and digestive systems that you have a soft and formed bowel movement at least daily. Your pooping patterns can be a good gauge for how well your body is supported by food and self-care choices.

Some other additive goals that I've personally used or seen clients have good experiences with are as follows: one or two additional home-cooked meals per week, increasing water intake, meal delivery services, and prepping food on Sundays so it's more readily available.

Satisfaction

Satisfaction is also important in deciding what to eat. When you eat foods that are more satisfying, you digest them better, so you're more likely to feel satiated. Fullness signals will also be more noticeable, making you less prone to eat beyond fullness or to feel that nibbling feeling that you just need more.

Many foods that are used in cultural celebrations or considered staples in some cultures are demonized due to an undercurrent of white supremacy in diet culture. For example, being told that you shouldn't eat tortillas with beans and rice because they "have too many carbs." If you cut out foods that are significant to your culture while under the influence of diet-culture, it can be powerful to reclaim those foods if you find them satisfying.

When you eat, your body is having a sensory experience. This experience is created through taste, touch, smell, and even memories. Therefore, the texture, temperature, appearance, and smell all contribute to this experience. How your body interprets the qualities of your food is unique for everyone. Your sensory experience of food can make a huge difference in the level of satisfaction, especially for neurodiverse folks. Eating food that's satisfying can help support nervous system regulation. If your nervous system is in a calm state, you'll digest your food better. If you're craving something crunchy, for example, it might support your sensory needs as well as enjoyment of your meal. Conversely, eating food that gives you a negative sensory experience can be dysregulating to your nervous system and leave you feeling unsatisfied.

I find that choosing satisfying foods also helps with feeling a stronger sense of agency around food and builds trust with your body. It's a physical action, affirming that you're listening to your body's signals and that your desires are valid. You're choosing your own discernment over a "should." This can be particularly challenging for people who are preoccupied and even harder for those who are anxious avoidant. Letting go of "shoulds" in favor of self-trust can feel scary. Go at the pace that feels good to you and get support if you need it.

If you've been restrictive, keep in mind that you might desire foods that have been off-limits. It's perfectly okay to have those foods and you'll likely find what satisfies you will shift after those foods lose their excitement.

Accessibility

It's also important to consider access. Having choice in what to eat is a privilege. Roughly 13% of US households experienced food insecurity in 2023 (U.S. Dept of Agriculture, 2025). If you're experiencing scarcity (or did at any point in your life), you may struggle more with feeling safe, feeling like there will be enough food, or feeling that it's okay to eat foods that are more expensive just because you like them. You might have pendulum swings between not wanting to spend money on food and splurging. There may be a food you ate during scarce times, like packs of ramen, that turns your stomach now.

If you have to choose foods that fit into a limited budget, or eat food provided by food banks, it can be helpful to be aware of how food scarcity has an impact on your relationship with food. This externally imposed restriction can be activating and cause eating patterns like bingeing when food is more readily available. It's really important to be gentle with yourself.

Living in a capitalist culture creates scarcity and oppression for many. I want to offer empathy and encouragement to blame the systems that put you and others in this position rather than taking on any shame for behaviors you may have around food that's caused by these systems. Get curious about what might be accessible and feel supportive to you as you navigate these experiences.

It's important to keep all of these factors in mind when considering what to eat. I hear over and over from folks, "I don't know what's wrong with me! I know what to eat, I just don't." This statement reflects the internalized shame of diet culture messaging. There is nothing wrong with you. There are very good reasons you don't eat what you've been told you "should."

Approaching food decisions in a secure way means using attunement and discernment. Time to get curious and start eating in a way that honors ALL of you.

When?

Our bodies like consistency. Eating every 3-5 hours when awake is helpful for blood sugar control, energy, gut health, and nervous system regulation. It's deeply supportive in building secure attachment with food, your*self*, and connection and trust with your body.

Eating regularly helps with body attunement; you'll notice patterns and feel your body's signals more strongly. Eating becomes an intentional act of caring for yourself by putting in nourishment multiple times a day and taking time to be in relationship with yourself. This builds trust, allowing your body to relax, knowing that its energy demands will be recognized and met.

If you have a history of restriction or lack, your body had to manage with less than it needed. It developed strategies to work around the deficit such as slowing your metabolism, and increasing or decreasing hunger, fullness, and satiety signals. Eating regularly tells your body it's safe to come out of survival mode.

If you aren't eating regularly, it's important to get curious about why and address the barriers to eating regularly. I find people with all three insecure attachment styles struggle to eat regularly.

One of the biggest reasons people cite is that their schedule doesn't allow it. Is that really true? Or is it that you're prioritizing work or other people's demands over your body's signals and needs? Why do you come last? It isn't your fault, there are reasons for those patterns... it's a survival strategy, but it's hurting you. I highly recommend using the 5A's back in Chapter 6, reading Chapter 9 on deep hunger, reading the book *Burnout* by Emily Nagoski and Amelia Nagoski, or getting coaching support around eating regularly.

Another reason you might not eat during the day is nervous system dysregulation. If you're constantly in fight-or-flight (sympathetic arousal), your body might not send hunger signals. In fight-or-flight, safety, not digestion, is the priority, so you probably won't feel like eating. If this is true for you, it's important to support your nervous system and address the underlying causes of your dysregulation.

A few years ago, I had a consultation with a high-powered business coach. She was worried that she was "overeating" at night. When I asked her to describe what she ate in a typical day, it turned out she was fasting before lunch, skipped lunch because of work stress, had back-to-back clients, and stopped eating at 7 or 8 p.m. because she heard it recommended on Oprah. So, for a couple of hours every evening, she would ravenously eat. Typically, she would feel overly full and have a lot of shame.

After exploring that pattern and understanding a bit more about primal hunger and nervous system dysregulation, she decided to make a change. She stopped intermittent fasting, created more space in her schedule, and prioritized eating during the day. After a few months, she updated me, saying how much less often she was eating beyond fullness at night and how much more energy she had during the day. She said, "Turns out I needed food! I deserve to make myself a priority. Who'd have thought!"

Yeah, but... I thought intermittent fasting was good for you.

It's restriction. It's just a diet with a trendy name. In the book *Food Isn't Medicine*,[28] Dr. Joshua Wolrich calls intermittent fasting privileged starvation. He goes on to quote the research that shows fasting to be a strong indicator of binge eating and bulimia.

Often, not eating regularly is a by-product of many of these complex layers: diet culture mentality, not feeling you can make yourself a priority, and stress. If you find it difficult to eat regularly after giving it a shot, you likely need more support to address any underlying issues. Additionally, if you're eating regularly but don't feel great physically, consider consulting a Registered Dietitian that uses a Health at Every Size® lens and is trained in Intuitive Eating, as this might be a symptom of nervous system dysregulation or digestive issues.

---

28. This title refers to the healthism claim that you can replace medication with eating your body weight in kale, or that if you eat "right," you won't experience illness. While I appreciate this book, I've personally stopped saying food isn't medicine. For many indigenous and other cultures, food is used medicinally. Healthism is appropriating this sacred practice.

Where?

Think of a time when you were sitting in a beautiful setting, enjoying a meal with people you love. Imagine the sights, the sounds, the way you felt, how satisfying the experience was.

Now think about eating while working away at your desk, standing in the kitchen, driving in your car, or eating while arguing with someone in your life. Did you even notice if you liked the food? Were you conscious of when you finished eating? Did you have an upset stomach after?

Whenever possible, eat in a place where your body and nervous system feel good. Cultivating an environment at home that feels supportive and enjoyable can be a great way to get into a nurturing self-care ritual while *eating*.

Do you have a dining room table? Is it covered with mail? No wonder you stand over the sink to eat. No judgment, I've been there.

One of my favorite things about my last home was that the dining room table overlooked the backyard and hummingbird feeder. I loved eating at the table, watching the birds flit about and the cycles of nature pass by. It can be so helpful and supportive to have a beautiful, relaxed environment to eat in.

At work, do you eat in front of your computer? I used to do this too. Unfortunately, it made mealtime feel like it almost didn't happen. It didn't make my stomach feel great either.

After practicing intuitive eating, I became much more aware of this pattern and how it affected me. At times, I still do eat at the computer or while driving someplace. But I now know I deserve to make it a priority to eat in peace, and I protect time for meals in my schedule.

Keep in mind that secure attachment uses structure as it's supportive. Don't beat yourself up if this is a challenge. Address any barriers you find to having a nice environment to eat in, such as over-working or prioritizing others' needs over your own. You may need to get support or resource yourself before making the changes you need.

Why?

There are so many reasons we eat, and they're all valid. I'm going to say that again: Every reason for eating is valid.

Seriously. And those reasons aren't solely valid for thin folks. Eating to soothe using food is valid; you're trying to get a need met. That's self-care. Eating for fun or nostalgia or celebration is valid and is self-care. Eating for hunger—even when you just ate an hour ago—is valid and is self-care. Eating in advance of getting hungry when you know you won't be able to eat at your normal time is valid and is self-care. I'm sure there are so many more reasons I haven't stated, but it's self-care.

Is it the "best" self-care in that moment? Maybe.

Eating what and why you want to WITHOUT shame is the best self-care you can give yourself. Again, honoring your agency and autonomy is so important and valuable in building connection and trust with yourself.

However, if you're eating in place of meeting an underlying need, that's only temporary support.[29]

Is soothing yourself temporarily useful? At times, yes. But the underlying need continues to go unmet. Patterns of self-avoidance might lead to ignoring your needs and using food to soothe. Folks who are securely attached honor the underlying needs whenever possible. If you struggle with this, remember, it isn't your fault nor something to judge yourself for. You'll work on this as you move toward secure attachment with your*self.* Be sure to read Chapter 8 on bingeing and Chapter 9 on deep hunger if this is an area of growth for you.

---

29. This might sound a little weird, but I think about this a lot: food is essentially the way we feel the inside borders of our bodies. Your digestive tract is a continuous tube that runs through the center of your body. Like a giant cannoli, lol. Ingesting food is frequently used as a surrogate for physical touch, which makes sense; it helps us connect to our bodies in a way that nothing else does.

*Every reason
for eating
is valid.*

How?

Eating at a pace that supports your digestion and your enjoyment is ideal. What's your ideal pace? It's different for everyone. Chewing your food thoroughly helps coat it in digestive enzymes, a key to breaking down food and absorbing more nutrients. Slowing down is better for digestion. And savoring your food leads to more enjoyment and increases satiety signals.

For many people, especially neurodivergent folks, you'll want a sensory specific environment. For you, trying to eat without distraction may make it *more* difficult to feel your body sensations. Similar to the way you can listen to a lecture better while doodling, having parts of your brain occupied may increase body attunement. You might need good music, a podcast, a fidget, company, or at least a nice view out the window. Experiment with what works best for you. The goal is to enjoy your meal while also tuning in to your body's signals when possible.

Please don't overwhelm yourself by trying to put all of these suggestions in place at once. Start with small, additive goals.

Do a resource assessment to see how you might resource yourself so you can focus on eating in a way that feels aligned and supportive of your overall wellbeing.

Does someone watch your kids after school? Maybe they can start dinner. Are you too tired after grocery shopping to cook? Ordering your groceries is one way to preserve your energy. Do you struggle most when you're hungry and don't have food easily available? Batch cooking one day a week might be a great way to support yourself in those times.

Start with a goal that feels very easy to achieve. Setting yourself up for success helps you believe in yourself more and creates momentum.

Break your goals down into baby steps. For example, if you want to start having family dinner at the table multiple nights a week but the dining room table is covered in papers, you might start with finding another space for a desk, asking a friend or partner to help you clear it off, or hiring an organizer to help you learn a better process for managing paper.

Remember, you're learning an entirely new way of relating to food and your body. Give yourself support, so much compassion, and know that it'll take time.

24-hour Recall, Self-Care Time, and Morning Practices

One of the coolest things about how our brains work is that practicing a new skill ANYTIME helps build the wiring to approach a challenging situation differently.

One of the ways I've found to support successful change is a 24-hour recall. This is not food tracking. I don't recommend food tracking as it can increase food preoccupation/anxiety and diet (restriction) behavior. I'd suggest using a 24-hour recall as structured time spent reviewing food patterns, behaviors, and body image issues that came up. You can review your eating patterns from the lens of some of the tools here, such as the 6W's and the hunger, fullness, and satiety scales, or look at particular areas of difficulty like bingeing, soothing using food, body avoidance, restrictive thinking, negative self-talk around food or body, etc.

The key here is curiosity.

Here are some questions that can be helpful when doing a 24-hour recall:

- What challenges did you experience with food and body image?
- What went well?
- What was happening before, during, and after?

- What sensations or feelings were coming up?
- How did I feel after I ate? Did I beat myself up?

The goal is to understand yourself better and find ways to support yourself to shift the underlying driver of the behavior or pattern. You're shining a spotlight of compassionate awareness on the behaviors, thoughts, and patterns you want to change. Don't attempt to stop the patterns or behaviors directly yet. If you do, the underlying issues most likely won't get addressed and you might return to the behaviors or patterns. Addressing any underlying causes helps the patterns and behaviors shift organically.

This is much easier if you already have time slotted for self-connection and self-reflection. I typically do this type of self-reflection during morning meditation or journaling. Meditation and many other practices have the added benefit of supporting your nervous system. I love achieving two goals at once!

I'm not going to prescribe a bunch of self-reflection practices; you likely have ideas about what you'd like to try or already know what works best for you. If you already have a routine, ritual, or practice, see if you can utilize that time by adding in reflection on food patterns and building skills for body connection and trust. If not, see if there's a new practice that feels easy to start with.

Whether you choose to do 24-hour recalls, morning pages, or other self-reflection practice(s), the most important thing is that it supports you! No "shoulds" allowed. If you do one for a while and fall off, there's a reason it isn't working. You might need to find additional ways to support yourself in doing the practice. It's also possible the new practice isn't as helpful as you hoped so you don't feel motivated to do it. That's okay. Let it go or find something different to try.

Having rituals, routines, and practices can be challenging, if not impossible, if you struggle with feeling you deserve to be a priority over other demands in your life. If you struggle to maintain your practices, get curious about why. If you notice that you're always putting others first, this may be part of your trauma/survival response. Rather than beating yourself up, get curious and begin to address why you don't feel you can be the priority.

It may also feel unsafe to sit in self-reflection. You may have so much internalized shame that when you check in with yourself, you're flooded with negative self-talk, causing your nervous system to freak out. Change isn't supported when you're experiencing deep shame and nervous system dysregulation. Change happens when we feel safe and resourced.

*It's not
your fault.*

Chapter Eight

Bingeing

I decided to devote an entire chapter to bingeing because it's the most common concern I hear. Bingeing impacts people of all sizes for many different reasons. When someone comes to me primarily concerned with binge eating, they typically feel so much shame. This shame makes it impossible to see your relationship with food and your body clearly.

Do you struggle with bingeing? Do you feel shame about it? Are you afraid there's something wrong with you because you binge?

The shame you hold about bingeing deepens the attachment wounds with yourself. Shame reinforces the false narrative that there's something wrong with you for having this behavior and disrupts trust in yourself and your body.

Bingeing isn't about being weak, out of control, or having no willpower. There's nothing wrong with you if you binge. Bingeing is simply a way to get a need met.

If you aren't getting enough food to meet your energy demands, your body will push you to eat as much as you can to make up for the perceived famine. If you're struggling with extreme stress levels, your body may drive you to eat to soothe your nervous system. If someone controlled what you were allowed to eat, and especially if you then tried to maintain their rules above your own needs and desires, your inner rebel will drive you to reclaim your autonomy by eating restricted food. If you're generally unsatisfied with life, food works as a way to feel satisfied, at least temporarily. If you lack human connection, you may binge to feel some kind of connection, or to soothe the deep pain from the lack of connection.

While bingeing does help you feel better in the short term, it doesn't feel great in the long term. Should you feel bad about that? No.

And still, bingeing only acts as a temporary balm. It doesn't actually address the underlying need. Having needs and desires go unmet long-term causes all kinds of pain and suffering. We'll discuss this further in the next chapter, "Deep Hunger."

So, what do we do about it?

Much of the difficulty with changing binge behaviors and patterns is the way you approach yourself. If you're trying to change from a place of shame because you think there's something wrong with you, it'll only cause more preoccupation, anxiety, or avoidance.

Want to change binge patterns? Start with getting clear on *why* you want to change them.

Is it to lose weight? It's unlikely that your size is due to bingeing. Equating bingeing with fatness is anti-fat bias. Many people who are fat don't binge, and many people who binge aren't fat. That assumption is diet culture rearing its ugly head. And again, diet culture tells us we need to change our body to be good enough. That approach stems from a place of thinking that there's something wrong with you for the way you are.

Conversely, if you're coming from a place of secure attachment, then your motive for changing a pattern stems from care and compassion for yourself rather than a "should" or shame. For example, you're wanting to change the bingeing pattern because it isn't meeting your deeper needs and isn't supporting your overall well-being. These would be securely attached reasons for wanting to change.

If shame is popping up, work on processing that first. You can't actually change your patterns of behavior if you're in shame about them, so wait until you're in a compassionate place and have addressed your shame. In that securely attached place, you'll have curiosity and compassion for yourself... and that's when change is possible!

> *You are not broken.*

Approaching bingeing from a place of secure attachment looks like first knowing that your value isn't diminished by this behavior. You are good. And you're struggling.[30]

First, you have to be in a place where you're ready for change—safe and resourced. Next is softening. This looks like noticing what's happening for you as you binge, bringing *awareness* to why you're bingeing, the circumstances surrounding it, and the feelings or sensations before, during, and after bingeing. Awareness shifts your unconscious behavioral patterns from unconscious incompetence to conscious incompetence.

Remember that judgment, aka shame, makes you feel unsafe and shuts the whole change process down. This is where acceptance comes in, accepting that you do binge and that's ok. Have curiosity and compassion for yourself rather than judgment.

Allowing the behavior to continue, rather than trying to control or manage it, helps increase awareness of the underlying patterns and allows your body to feel safe. If you think you must stop

---

30. This language was inspired by the book *Good Inside* by Dr. Becky Kennedy. It's a parenting book that I recommend. She reminds us over and over that your child is a good kid having a hard time. Imagine if your parents ingrained that in you when you were young. You ARE good, you're just having a hard time.

yourself anytime you notice you're about to binge, you'll likely avoid awareness around it so that you can still binge. If this is how you've been getting your needs partially met, trying to control the behavior only results in not getting the needs met. Eventually, you'll start bingeing again or desperately seek other ways to get the need met. You have to experience the patterns surrounding the behavior over and over to understand what's needed to shift it. Once you understand what your underlying needs are, you can address them directly. For example, if you're soothing loneliness with food, try to seek out companionship. As you meet the need, the desire to binge will naturally diminish.

Practicing *acknowledgment* can be really powerful in making peace with bingeing. In making peace with bingeing, you can release shame and negative self-talk (which only work against you). I like to think of it this way: your body found a way to keep you alive as best as it knows how. It's been scrappy and has resourced you despite lack. Thank you, body!

There's nothing wrong with bingeing, and still, you deserve more attuned and responsive care. Your body and nervous system need additional support, more self-care options, and more ways of truly getting your needs met. As you meet your underlying needs, you will rely on bingeing less.

Even as you start to care for yourself in a more attuned and responsive way, you might find that you still binge. This is really common. Remember that bingeing is a survival strategy. You may need to re-establish safety using this well-oiled behavior (bingeing). Your brain and body might simply need to know that it's still an option. This is part of the change process, not a sign of failure. This is when you begin to have conscious competence.

Continue building that connection and trying new ways of supporting yourself, and accordingly, the need to rely on bingeing will diminish. If you're finding it challenging to let go of shame and to approach yourself with curiosity, or if you're practicing this system and it feels like you aren't making progress, you may need to seek professional support.

Step by Step:

For those of you who prefer a structured list, here are the steps I recommend if you're struggling with binge eating:

1. Start by eating food throughout the day. Make sure you're no longer restricting.
2. Get curious about why you want to change the bingeing pattern and behaviors.
3. Address underlying shame and feelings of "not enough."
4. Find your motivation from a place of compassion.
5. Resource yourself.
6. Practice the 5A's.
7. With curiosity and compassion, bring awareness to the behaviors, patterns, sensations, and feelings around bingeing.
8. Have acceptance, allow the patterns, and feel the feelings.
9. Listen to what your body is signaling; what are your underlying need(s)?
10. Honor those underlying needs (more about this in the next section).

Notice that I didn't say anything about controlling the behavior or trying to white-knuckle it. The goal isn't to stop bingeing. The goal is to support yourself the best you can. Bingeing is a valid tool, but it isn't the only tool. Let's develop more tools; having options is so valuable.

Chapter Nine

Deep Hunger

When I started writing this chapter, I felt stuck. Deep hunger felt so big. One day, business coach Kate Holly sent out an email with some journal prompts, starting with a question by Audre Lorde that inspired me: "What are the words you do not have yet?"

Here are my reflections:

I don't have the words to heal the ache
because the ache is so deep.

There's no end to it, only layers and tendrils.
It's beautiful, really, yet daunting.

How do you start when you know you can't finish?

When you want to show them how to get to
where you are, navigate where you've been, but
you have no idea where you're going?

At the same time, I know deep down it's magical that
I have no idea where I'm going. That's freedom.

> *Where I was headed before was predictable*
> *and tragic, but now I have so much possibility.*
>
> *I used to push my aches away. I tried to deny*
> *them, and I tried to make the world hurt me less*
> *by changing who I was. But now I know it isn't*
> *the number or depth of the aches, but what you*
> *do with them, how you live with them, how you*
> *feel and honor them that makes the difference.*
>
> *It's the process of relating to yourself, to your*
> *aches, in which freedom and possibility live.*
>
> *As I find my words, I hope they'll guide you to your*
> *aches, to freedom, and to all the possibilities.*

Deep Hunger: Unmet Needs

When you're deeply hungry for basic human social needs, food may be a way to dull the ache. You might use food to soothe or disconnect from your body. You might attempt to control your body and food intake because it gives you a sense of safety, or because you're striving to gain access to those unmet needs (thinness equals conditional acceptance in our society). You might've even learned to simply ignore your body's signals that something important is missing. But nothing other than acknowledging and meeting those needs as best you can will ultimately bring contentment and satisfaction.

> "The body is a source of wisdom that needs to be understood.
> Eating disorder behaviors are the body speaking about how it
> makes sense of life, what it takes to be alive, and what the soul
> needs to thrive."
>
> —Embodied Recovery for Eating Disorders

*When we honor
our hunger
on a physical,
emotional, and
spiritual level, we
can build trust
with our bodies.*

The issue here isn't that you're using food in a way that doesn't align with how you'd like to use food. The issue is that you're deeply hungry for something else. Trying to control or manage food will never work. Getting your deeper needs met is the best way to support yourself in changing patterns that no longer align and in becoming securely attached with food, your body, and yourself. Once these needs are met, your desire or need to eat in a way that isn't aligned will naturally diminish.

What do you hunger for the most?

What does your soul ache for?

What have you been without for so long that you're almost numb to it?

Do you long to feel safe and accepted?

To belong?

Do you wish you could finally be seen and heard? Do you wish for understanding?

For stability? For love?

Do you long to have a greater impact?

To dance? To play?

Do you know you deserve it all?

Controlling food or your body may bring you more social acceptance. For some, pursuing intentional weight loss brings conditional
social acceptance and thin privilege. For others, social acceptance
can make a difference in how safe they are, especially fat BIPOC
folks and those with intersecting marginalized identities.

I'm not the best person to decide if pursuing thinness or controlling food to attempt to gain acceptance is worth it; you are. Here
are a few questions to help you get some clarity around the reasons
it's been hard for you to let go of trying to fit in.

- What is the cost of accepting yourself as you are?
- What is the cost of attempting to control food and your body?

For most, at minimum, attempting to control food and your
body requires overriding your body's signals. This causes a loss of
your sense of agency and autonomy. It can activate your inner rebel.
For most people, it adds to the internalized message that you aren't
good enough as you are. It erodes trust in yourself.

Diet culture teaches us that we need to try harder to control or
manage food and our bodies, that we have to try harder to fit in. For
most people, the cost of trying to fit in is too high. It's the cost of a
secure relationship with themselves. In addition to being extremely
painful, it typically doesn't work to try to control your body (diets
don't work). Dieting isn't worth it.

Rather than beating yourself up for your behavior and patterns
around food and body, or trying to control yourself harder, focus on
exploring what's missing that's leading to these patterns.

How Do You Learn What Your Underlying Needs Are?

One of the best ways to learn what you're deeply hungry for, what
underlying needs are beneath your challenges with food and your

body, is to regularly spend time in self-reflection with curiosity and compassion. Use self-reflection time to look for patterns around unmet needs and get clarity using your body sensations and body wisdom as a guide. The 5A's can be a powerful daily self-reflection tool, but use what works best for you.

Coaches and somatic practitioners can be very helpful for discovery around deeper needs and desires. I love this question from Tuck Malloy, an awesome relationship coach, certified holistic sex educator, and MFT therapist in training: "What would I most like to hear or experience in this moment?" The answer might be difficult to find at first. It's normal to feel awkward or unsure, or even scared.[31]

Try to find and listen to the small, quiet, vulnerable parts of you. If you come up with nothing, that's okay. Try thinking of a child, like a niece or nephew, and think about what kind of support you think they'd deserve in a similar situation to yours. Or try thinking of someone dear to you that provided words or experiences that felt supportive (at any point in your life): a partner, a family member like a grandmother or auntie, a teacher, etc.

This might be activating if you never had someone supportive in your life. Please know that a lack of care only means you deserve this love and support even more. You may need to grieve the loss of the care you deserved growing up (and now). Consider doing this work with a therapist or support group. For now, play with making up a character, watch for someone kind and caring in movies, or witness a caregiver caring for a child while you're out in the world.

Once you have a supportive person in mind, think about how their actions were caring. Try giving yourself those kind words or

---

31. The first time I tried this was in a conflict with a partner. I heard a small voice inside telling me that I just wanted to hear that they love me. I felt so vulnerable. I could barely acknowledge it and definitely couldn't tell them. Now I'm well-practiced and embrace those messages—they guide me through life and bring me closer to the life and relationships I want.

actions. Stay curious about what might feel supportive and experiment with it. Notice how it feels. It might feel awkward to receive support from yourself, so it might not feel great immediately. Practice giving and receiving support to and from yourself. When you get more clarity about what you'd like to feel or experience, what you desire, and what truly feels like support, you'll be able to practice asking for support and for your needs to be met from those who feel safe in your life.

At times, learning to give your*self* the things you're hungry for will be all you need. Some needs, like physical safety, belonging, and acceptance, might be helped by giving them to yourself or finding ways to incorporate them into your life as best you can, but as social beings, you need to receive them from others as well to feel deeply fed.

If you never received what felt like good support from caregivers or others in your life, you may struggle to figure out what actually feels supportive. At times, you may reach for what you think you want, and it won't feel good. This can be because it feels foreign to have the thing you've longed for but never experienced. Or it could be because what you thought you wanted wasn't it. Understanding what feels nurturing to you (as you are right now) and learning to receive are two different steps.

If you've been lacking in support, attempting to get support may feel scary. This is true for any unmet need. If a need has gone unmet for a long time, you may have shut it down to avoid feeling the pain of it being unmet. There will be a period of learning that it's safe to want the need to be met, to desire it, and to reach for it. You may have grief built up over the lack of that need being met, making it even more difficult to reach for the need or even acknowledge it. You might notice a tendency to avoid the need in order to avoid feeling the grief. Be sure to give yourself so much compassion, spaciousness, and grace as you explore.

Needs

Here's a short list of some of the things I see missing for many clients (and many that were missing for me):

- water
- food
- shelter
- safety
- acceptance
- connection
- touch
- being seen
- purpose
- satisfaction
- creative expression
- pain relief
- trauma healing
- agency
- autonomy

- justice
- support
- feeling enough
- pleasure
- novelty
- adventure
- time in nature
- spaciousness
- boundaries
- sexual expression
- stability
- financial security
- play
- care
- gender expression

Make a list of the needs on this list (and beyond) that you currently feel you have enough of. These are reminders of what fulfilled needs feel like; you can lean on the experience of these fulfilled needs as you navigate this learning. You can also use the needs that are already met as resources to support yourself in seeking unmet needs. For example, if you have financial security, you can understand what security feels like. You can also use your financial security to pay for coaching or other supports in reaching for unmet needs.

Next, make a list of the needs you feel are lacking. It can be helpful to look at each need as it pertains to your relationship with yourself, and as it pertains to community or relationships with others. For example, you may feel you see yourself deeply but don't feel seen with others, or the reverse may be true... you may have a loved one who really sees you, but you may have so much shame and self-doubt clouding your view that you don't feel you see or understand *yourself.*

Awareness is the first step. Curiosity and experimenting with how to get these needs met is next. But there are often barriers to seeing and reaching for them. We'll explore that next.

For now, remember...

It's not your fault.

You are not broken.

I believe in you.

Chapter Ten

Barriers to Body Attunement and Healing

There are many barriers to body attunement and reaching for deep underlying needs to be met. It's important to acknowledge and support yourself around these barriers. Many people view difficulty with learning body attunement and intuitive eating as a personal flaw. The belief that "if you're struggling, it's your fault" only results in more shame and will keep you stuck. Instead of shaming yourself, it's time to get curious.

Here are the most common barriers I see.

Systems of Oppression and Inequality

In a world that's often unsafe for fat people, and especially those with additional marginalized identities, such as disabled people, BIPOC, and LGBTQIA2s+ people, it can be difficult and potentially dangerous to go against cultural expectations by refusing to pursue weight loss.

There are many consequences for not pursuing thinness, or not trying to make your body fit in. The cultural ladder of bodily hierarchy, as Sonya Renee Taylor calls it in *The Body is Not an Apology,* creates layers and layers of discrimination. For some people, if they do go against social expectations, it literally means death.

From the Harvard College website on systems of oppression (this quote appears to have been removed as of April 2025, a creepy sign of the times):

"Racism. Heterosexism. Ableism. Sexism. Colonialism. Transphobia. These are just a few of the pervasive 'Systems of Oppression' that sustain deep imbalances in power, wealth, and opportunity, fueling profoundly disparate health outcomes within and between communities.

Health inequities are sustained across a myriad of outcomes— maternal mortality, average life expectancy, chronic disease burden, COVID-19 infection and death rates, injury or death from police brutality. Such disparities don't stem from twists of fate, genetics, nor solely are they the consequences of habits or lifestyle. Rather, long-standing, intersectional systems of oppression can put individuals at higher risk for contracting certain conditions, can disrupt critical physiological processes essential to maintaining good health and deprive individuals and communities of critical health protective resources." (Harvard College, 2024)

I find this to be a helpful way to frame the impact of our cultural systems of oppression, and yet, this statement discusses health disparities, but weight stigma isn't included. This is an example of how an entire group of people are left out of the conversation on matters directly and significantly impacting them, and therefore, they're harmed further.

Fat people have less access to healthcare, receive worse healthcare treatment, and accordingly, frequently have worse health outcomes. Fat people are likely to earn less and are given fewer job offers than their thin counterparts. In the United States, where healthcare is tied to employment and costs a significant amount of money to access, being under-employed directly influences access to healthcare.

Even when healthcare cost isn't a factor, anti-fat bias and weight stigma in our healthcare system leads to a lack of access for people in larger bodies. If you know you'll be shamed by doctors, you'll be prone to healthcare avoidance. And when people override that fear and go anyway, many fat people have their very real symptoms ignored. Instead of getting the same treatment as thin people, they're told they need to lose weight. This leads to a lack of appropriate treatment plans and even premature death.

In her book *Weightless*, Evette Dionne writes of treatment she received as the result of gaining weight rapidly as a girl. Her doctors encouraged her parents to put her on a diet when she was 10. She was also teased relentlessly and regularly touched inappropriately by the other kids in her class. Her school did nothing to protect her. She described it as being an object in a world in which her body is not her own.

Some people are granted bodily autonomy (thin, "healthy," white, cis-gendered men) and everyone else is on a sliding, conditional scale—conditional on the approval of the dominant class. With each intersecting marginalized identity, especially for superfat+ people, the lack of autonomy and safety risk increases.

Dionne goes on to share the statistic that "ob*se" children are 65% more likely to be teased than children in the "normal" (bogus) BMI category. (Bogus) BMI, our healthcare system, our legislation, and the "fight against obesity" all perpetuate the harmful messages that fat people are less than. Children consistently receive the message that there's something wrong with being fat, that being fat isn't normal, and that it's okay to treat fat people badly, leading to bullying.

Being constantly torn down by your peers is a nightmare no person should have to endure. It's dehumanizing and creates painful social isolation. For most, unconsciously, it's easier to believe there's something wrong with themselves and try to fit in than to believe and accept that so many other people are wrong. And that so many other people—often their friends, parents, and professionals they trust—would be so hurtful.

This leads to internalization one of two messages: something is wrong with me so I should try to change it, or there's something that others think is so wrong with me that I'll get treated less than (or potentially even be killed) for being this way.

This leads to shame, trauma, a dysregulated nervous system, and deep attachment ruptures.

White Lens

In the United States, our culture is largely influenced by colonization and white supremacy. It's all I've ever known. I've had to actively seek out ways to unlearn and see things differently. And yet, because I've drowned in these systems and messaging my whole life, I'm only able to write a book from the perspective of someone who had/has this conditioning.

This conditioning is a barrier to body attunement. Seeing yourself from a lens that says some people are better than others pits us against not only one another, but also the parts of us that we deem less than—the parts we're afraid to see or have seen. These perceived imperfections are important parts of who we are. They show us what we want, what parts of us need love and healing, and what simply needs to be embraced as part of who we are. When you reject parts of yourself through the white lens, you miss the opportunity of deeply knowing yourself.

This is one reason it's so important to seek out resources written from people who have had different experiences. It's also why it's important to take responsibility for unlearning and give yourself compassion if you haven't fully grasped these concepts or if they are new to you. If you're Black, Indigenous, a person of color, and/or hold other marginalized identities impacted by systems of oppression, please know I see the extra work and emotional labor you have to do to filter books written from the white lens to apply them to your experience. Take these ideas and make them work for you and reject the ones that don't.

Shame

Shame stems from thinking you ARE bad—inherently, or because of something you've done. Guilt is a feeling that often stems from doing something that doesn't align with your personal values or an outside expectation, a "should"—not from believing you're bad.

Western culture and many others around the world use shame as a form of punishment and in an attempt to mold or control behaviors. Using shame as a way of trying to change behaviors that don't fit with the desired cultural norms doesn't work and is harmful.

Shame only inhibits someone from performing visible behaviors. It doesn't change the root of why they're doing the behavior in the first place (hint: there's an underlying need going unmet). This is why people in recovery so often experience the addiction whack-a-mole.

It also doesn't work because many of our cultural norms aren't healthy in the first place, essentially shaming people into denying their basic human needs like autonomy, connection, nurturance, sustenance, and self-acceptance.

White supremacy shames people for the color of their skin, their socioeconomic status, weight/size/(bogus)BMI, physical appearance, physical ability, IQ, sexual orientation, gender expression, and the list goes on.

Though subtle, ordinary social pressure is a powerful (and painful) motivator, and the systems of oppression are even more insidious. Our culture wields shame as a weapon, attempting to force people to deny who they are and hate themselves for not falling in line with the "ideal." This is to keep the unequal power balance in place and make those with marginalized identities powerless.

We internalize these messages and pass them on from generation to generation in an attempt to keep ourselves and our children safe. We attempt to keep our children in line so they won't be rejected or harmed, but it perpetuates the wiring that it's dangerous to be oneself and seek out acceptance as we are.

Many professionals in the body-positive eating disorder recovery spaces don't account for the environment you live in. There are so many messages that simply say, eat the donut, love your body—without accounting for the real-life dangers of doing so, more for some than others.

Deep healing isn't possible if you think it's just about your own mindset. This is why it's so important to acknowledge how our systems and cultural messages created your mindset.

Some shame is identity-based, and some is action-based. You might feel you deserve to be ashamed as the result of something you have or haven't done. Shame is a barrier to body attunement, self-acceptance, and secure attachment.

I've worked with many clients who felt unworthy of self-acceptance due to something they did. They felt their behavior was so wrong that they couldn't possibly forgive themselves. This pent-up shame prevented them from feeling they deserved to be prioritized, loved, accepted, or able to trust themselves.

You may also feel shame for harm you caused due to old belief systems, such as upholding white supremacy, participating in body shaming, or promoting diets. While you didn't intend to cause harm, impact matters more than intent. The good news is you now understand that those behaviors harm others and you can change. The bad news is that if you continue to shame yourself, it'll be more difficult to change, and to have a loving, attuned relationship with yourself. You *deserve* a loving, attuned relationship with yourself. Even if you hurt people or hurt yourself (we all have).

Shame thrives on a lack of self-forgiveness. Some of the reasons listed by clients who said they couldn't forgive themselves were: stealing, lying, having an affair, driving drunk or high, harming someone while driving drunk, having an abortion, not speaking up about abuse, having an eating disorder, hiding while eating, abusing drugs, harming a child, making big mistakes at work, putting their child on a diet, saying something racist, and the list goes on.

When I started looking at my shame, I had some very difficult things to face. I found Brené Brown's book *I Thought It Was Just Me (But It Isn't)* and Kristin Neff's work on self-compassion to be helpful in working through it. I went through the phases of trauma healing and spent a lot of time grieving and learning to accept myself, mistakes and all.

Here's the affirmation that helped me the most. I said it to myself multiple times a day until I felt the shame start to diminish:

> *"The person I was at that moment in time did the best I could with the skills and capacity I had. Today, I'm a different person and I'm learning new ways of navigating challenges."*[32]

Yeah, but... I could have done better!

Could you have? If you were in pain and didn't know how to get through it, or if you were careless and made a poor split-second decision, or if you were angry and lashing out... I still believe that you didn't have a better way of coping during that time or

---

32. I adapted this but couldn't find the source. If it is yours, thank you!

navigating that situation. If you did have the capacity, skills, or ability, you would've done it differently. Making a bad choice doesn't make you bad.

I've heard some people say, "I can't let myself off the hook." Forgiving yourself is NOT the same as letting yourself off the hook. In fact, forgiveness allows you to release shame so you can take responsibility for your past actions and learn how to resource yourself so you can do better going forward.

Consider these questions:
- What do I feel I can't forgive myself for?
- If a friend told me they'd done the same thing, how would I respond to them?
- How might my life be different if I forgave myself for those things?
- How does the shame I hold about those things impact my life and those around me?
- What will it take to forgive myself?
- Is there a way I can make amends that would allow me to let go of my shame?

Telling someone safe about your shame can be extremely helpful in working through it as well. Be sure to resource yourself as you do this work.

Shame is possibly the biggest barrier to secure attachment with yourself, body attunement, and discovering your underlying needs that aren't being met. The feeling that you're bad, wrong, or not good enough as you are creates deep wounds and makes secure attachment with yourself feel impossible. Working through shame can support you in knowing in your bones that you're good enough, valuable, and worthy of love and respect as you are. Doing this work is so powerful!

Achievement Energy

Have you ever said you're your #1 priority? Try it now.

> *I am my priority.*

How does it feel? What are the sensations that come up in your body? Do you feel sheepish? Does it feel selfish? If so, why?

Unless you have a brand-new baby and are a single parent, there's no reason you shouldn't be your #1 priority. If not you, who will make you the priority?

Being your top priority doesn't mean you won't do good work in the world or care for others. I've found that prioritizing myself has freed me to give in ways that are aligned with how I want to give, and that don't require me to override my body. It did mean some changes: letting go of certain relationships, leaving a job that was exhausting me and leaving me feeling unfulfilled and letting go of people pleasing, for example. Those choices were, at times, extremely hard, but culling the people, places, and things that drained me—that didn't have my best interest at heart—was freeing. It allowed me to have the relationships, lifestyle, and work that are right for me.

My dear friend, intuitive mentor, and author Jennifer Crews introduced me to achievement energy: being overly focused on accomplishments or "shoulds." It was one of the biggest barriers to making myself the priority, to listening to my body and honoring the deeper needs I was missing. Achievement energy drove me to ignore my body and do the things I thought I needed to do to be accepted and valued by others (Brené Brown calls this hustling for your worth). Eventually, I was able to dismantle those internalized messages that I was only good enough if I looked a certain way, ate a certain way, made others happy, was productive enough, etc.

My core belief is that everyone is inherently valuable and worthy of love and respect. From this belief, I'm able to be securely attached with myself. I'm able to do the work that lights me up. I'm able to release shame because I know that my value isn't dependent on being perfect. Here's a womanifesto[33] I wrote that reflects this belief.

> *I believe...*
> *We are each valuable and*
> *worthy of love and respect,*
> *no matter what.*
>
> *Our value and worth can't be reduced*
> *to our genitals, how we look, or*
> *what the scale says today.*
>
> *It can't be reduced by how many things we*
> *checked off our to-do list, whether we did*
> *all the "shoulds,"or what we ate today.*
>
> *Our value isn't determined by how many*
> *hours we've worked, what we struggle*
> *with, or how our bodies function today.*
>
> *It can't be judged by whether we're a*
> *"good" child, sibling, or spouse; whether*
> *we want children, whether we have*
> *them, or how we choose to rear them.*

33. I took a womanifesto workshop at Camp Yes! (a fun and impactful summer camp for femme leaders) put on by coach Marli Williams. Since there were no men there, doing a (wo)manifesto workshop made more sense.

> *Knowing our value is constant, and that we*
> *are worthy of love and respect, no matter what,*
> *creates a ripple effect within us.*
>
> *This ripple expands outside of our*
> *depths, meeting the shore, where we*
> *help others to know they too are worthy*
> *of love and respect, no matter what.*

When I started working with people as a Certified Intuitive Eating Professional, I saw that my clients also needed to shift the old wiring that they're only good enough if they look or act a certain way. This was a big piece of the puzzle for many in healing their relationship with food and body. When they prioritized other things and people above themselves, they couldn't be attuned to and honor their bodies, needs, or desires.

One client, who I adore, discovered she had the subconscious belief that her value was tied to being the responsible one in her family. So, if she ate cereal for dinner, she felt like she wasn't responsible because she wasn't being "healthy enough." Or if she used food to soothe, she'd feel like she'd failed at being responsible and would beat herself up. But at the same time, she craved letting go of that constant vigilance and just having something easy, fun, and familiar for dinner.

These parts of herself were in conflict, leading to shame and frustration, which only made her want to soothe using food even more. This also activated her inner rebel, making her want to say, "F it all." She'd avoid doing the things that made her feel like she was taking care of herself, again adding to the feeling that she wasn't being responsible enough.

She's done so much work to shift the belief that her value is based in caring for others and now knows she's inherently valuable.

Since I mention "inner rebel," please know your inner rebel is NOT trying to sabotage you. Your inner rebel isn't something to be pushed around, ignored, or hated. It's a part of you. It's screaming for autonomy, to be heard, seen, acknowledged. If you're in an energy deficit, it might just be screaming for enough food. It's trying to keep you alive and well.

Your value and worth have nothing to do with your appearance, what you eat, or how much you fit into the cultural beauty norms. It's not based on your achievements, how much you got checked off your to-do list, or who you made happy today.

Yeah, but... doesn't it matter how I show up? Aren't I more valuable if I look good or do good things in the world?

Nope. This is hustling for your worth. Try this exercise.

Answer the following with your inner dialogue voice (you know, the one with the judgy tone that you prefer to keep to yourself, the one you'd never use to talk to your friend but use with yourself all the time):

- What makes me "good," lovable, and enough?
- How do I try to prove to others that I'm good?
- What are my good qualities?
- Who do I feel I have to prove myself to? How do I do that?

Now take a few deep breaths and switch into curiosity mode:

- What makes a human valuable?
- How would your life look different if you knew, in your bones, that you're inherently valuable?

If you're finding your answer to human value is what you DO, not that you simply ARE, consider people you love. If they were suddenly incapacitated in some way, and couldn't DO anything for you, would you still love them? If you've experienced loving a child, did your love require them to do anything or be any particular way?

Why doesn't that kind of love apply to you?

> "Human Giver Syndrome—the contagious belief that you have a moral obligation to give every drop of your humanity in support of others, no matter the cost to you—thrives in the patriarchy, the way mold thrives in damp basements."
>
> **—Emily Nagoski, PhD, and Amelia Nagoski, DMA,** *Burnout: The Secret to Unlocking the Stress Cycle*

Yep, it's patriarchy and capitalism and anti-fat bias all rolled into one steaming heap of moldy shame. In the book *Burnout*, Emily Nagoski and Amelia Nagoski frame this as Human Giver Syndrome. Pouring your energy out in an attempt to be accepted in our culture, to gain some security, leaves many people with few resources left for themselves. As suggested in *Burnout*, remember: the game is rigged. Calling out systems of oppression and inequality as responsible for burnout is helpful. Remember that it's not your fault, the system is designed to set you up to fail.

It's not your fault.
You are not broken.

Exploring your relationship with achievement energy can go a long way in bringing you to secure attachment with yourself AND having a more satisfying life.

Physical Barriers

If you're struggling to build body attunement, it's important to consider that you may have barriers that go beyond cultural conditioning or a lack of body attunement skills. Looking for physical barriers can be the difference between success and failure with intuitive eating. Pinpointing barriers can provide relief from self-judgment as well as a starting point for what to focus your energy on, rather than thinking that there's something wrong with you and spinning your wheels. There's a big difference between "something is wrong that I need support with" and "there's something wrong with me." Alcohol/substance abuse or challenges, pain, being a highly sensitive person (HSP), anxiety, depression, sensory processing disorders, and neurodivergence are some possible physical barriers to body attunement.

If you have any of these challenges and they're making learning body attunement skills difficult, start by resourcing yourself around those barriers. I'll sound like a broken record in this chapter. Get professional help if you struggle with any of these or if you're struggling to build body attunement. There's likely more to the story than you can see.

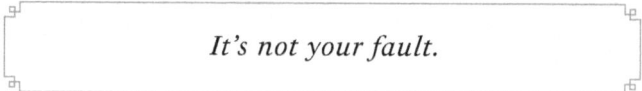

It's not your fault.

Substance/Alcohol Misuse

This barrier is near and dear to my heart. I'm in recovery from alcohol and substance use disorder.[34] Many of my clients are as well. It's extremely common to have co-occurrence—both having an eating

---

34. I recently celebrated 27 years alcohol and substance free! I choose to recover out loud to help others know that recovery is possible.

disorder and struggling with substances. Per the National Eating Disorders Collaboration website, up to 50% of patients with an eating disorder will abuse alcohol or an illicit substance, compared with 9% of the population (Gregorowski et al., 2013). Further, individuals with eating disorders are up to five times likelier to abuse alcohol or illicit drugs, and those who abuse alcohol or illicit drugs are up to 11 times likelier to have eating disorders (The National Center on Addiction and Substance Abuse at Columbia University, 2003).

Alcohol and substances provide a barrier to feeling sensations in your body. Having that barrier on occasion isn't usually a big issue. But when you're frequently using alcohol or substances, you become very disconnected from your body and its signals. For some, seeking disconnection is the reason or driver for abusing alcohol and substances. It may have felt too painful to be in your body. Typically, people who struggle with alcohol and substances have a history of adverse childhood experiences and trauma, so if this is your experience, there are likely painful feelings that are still unresolved.

If you struggle with alcohol and/or substance use, seek support. One of my favorite support groups for femme and non-binary people is SHE RECOVERS®. They welcome people in recovery from alcohol, substances, over-working, trauma, cancer, and beyond, and they honor all pathways of recovery. I also recommend checking out these recovery programs: Love Sober and Soberful. They each have tremendously supportive online communities, podcasts, and offer coaching services.

When you stop using alcohol and substances, it can often result in feeling overwhelmed by sensations you've had all along but have been dulled. Be sure to give yourself time and resource yourself before diving headfirst into feeling all the things at once. Work on slowly building tolerance for sitting with the sensations in your body and your feelings. This is such a big part of recovery and so rewarding in building a secure relationship with yourself.

Anxiety and Depression

Suffering from anxiety and/or depression makes it very difficult to feel safe in your body. Your body's perception of threat is increased, and the nervous system is often dysregulated, causing a cascade of hormones like cortisol, increasing your allostatic load (the stress or wear and tear on your body). Part of your body is setting off alarm bells, while the rest of you is just trying to get through the day. This internal battle becomes a central focus for your mind and body, making it difficult to prioritize building body attunement.

It's physically painful for many sufferers as well. When you're in pain, it's very difficult to want to go toward those feelings—those uncomfortable signals blaring in your body.

There's a high correlation between anxiety, depression, and eating disorders/disordered eating (and alcohol/substance abuse as well).[35] This is because the drivers that predispose people to one also predispose people to the others. Factors like trauma, adverse childhood experiences, genetic history, and even birth trauma can all contribute to these lasting issues.

You may have developed eating patterns in response to anxiety or depression as a survival strategy: eating to soothe, not eating to feel safe, etc. People who have a higher rate of anxiety and depression tend to struggle with digestion as well, leading to eating patterns that try to mitigate discomfort.

"Anxiety is like a persistent child. She will demand your attention, usually in very unpleasant ways, until you meet her needs."
—**Katherine Kozioziemski, somatic anxiety coach**

There are so many layers to how and why challenges with anxiety and depression are barriers to body attunement and intuitive eating. The good news is that getting support and treatment for those

---

35. I'm a triple winner myself!

challenges will also support you in your relationship with food and your body. The other good news is that many of the tools in this book will also help you cope with anxiety and depression. Ironically, it's often exactly the feelings and sensations that we're trying to avoid or move away from that need our attention the most. It might be counterintuitive, but bringing awareness to, accepting, and allowing those parts of you to be heard is often the solution.

If you're struggling with anxiety and/or depression, know that I understand how hard it is. There's no right way to navigate through these struggles besides your way—the way that feels accessible to you. Start wherever you can and give yourself so much grace.

I believe in you.

Pain

Feeling chronic pain makes it extremely difficult to feel safe or comfortable focusing on the sensations present in your body. It also can lead to chronic dysregulation of your nervous system. When you're constantly activated, remembering to or feeling safe enough to check in with your body isn't going to be a priority. Pain is an alert from your body; it's usually much louder than the rest of the signals in your body. This makes it difficult to feel anything else.

If you have chronic pain, please attempt to get support. Seek ways to reduce or manage your pain. I know from personal experience it can be really hard to try one more thing when you feel that you've tried it all and nothing worked. Keep going!

Along with working on reducing or managing your pain, begin to focus on things other than pain. When you do a body scan, note the pain, then scan your body for areas that feel pleasant or neutral. Or if your pain seems to be everywhere, look for areas that are less painful than the rest, and explore those sensations. When your body feels alright for a day, an hour, or even a few minutes, focus on increasing awareness of what that feels like.

Do your best to resource yourself with things that remind your nervous system that you're safe. Try to keep in mind that your pain, while important, isn't an emergency (this only applies to chronic pain that isn't an emergency, that you've explored the medical reasons for—not acute, unexplained pain). There is more happening in your body than pain. The goal is to broaden your awareness to include all of you so that your pain isn't all-consuming.

Highly Sensitive Person

Being a highly sensitive person (HSP) is unique and significant; you're tuned in to the subtler signals in the world. HSPs tend to be very open to the world around them, having very porous boundaries. It can feel overwhelming and even painful to feel everything so intensely. So, hearing me ask you throughout this book to feel even more might seem like a terrible idea. For you, it isn't about feeling more, but about using discernment in what *you* feel vs taking on feelings outside of you. Then determining the best way to navigate the world based on your needs.

It's important to recognize how your body takes in sensory input and how that impacts you in the day-to-day. It can be so valuable to prioritize creating a supportive lifestyle and habits. You might work from home, skip events in intense environments, or make sure you have good recovery time when needed. Implementing even a few strategies to support your needs goes a long way. Discovering what's activating and choosing what to (and what not to) engage with can be helpful… but it might not be possible to control your environment enough to reduce the stress to the level that feels like you're safe consistently. Developing great self-care habits is very important to cope with the inevitable stress on your body from processing all that input.

Lastly, focus on increasing your internal and external boundaries. This will allow you to take on more of what truly matters to you and less of what doesn't bring satisfaction. It'll also help you to feel sovereign and safer in your body. Boundaries help with building body attunement to yourself, rather than your environment or people around you.

Reducing the incoming stressors and supporting yourself to manage the stress that does come in will free up space and energy to become more attuned to your body. It'll also help your body and nervous system to trust that it's safe to prioritize tuning in to your internal world. If you are a highly sensitive person or suspect you might be, it is so important to get non-shaming, affirming support. When you can, seek out professionals who are specifically trained in supporting HSPs, and peers who have personal experience with HSP.

My body is my home, my ally, not my enemy.

Sensory Processing Disorders

"Sensory Processing Disorder (SPD) is a neurological condition that interferes with the body's ability to receive messages from the senses and convert those messages into appropriate motor and behavioral responses"

—ADDitude Magazine, 2025

Having sensory processing or integration disorder can make the world harder to navigate. It can cause overwhelm and difficulty interpreting the signals coming in. "Pioneering occupational therapist, psychologist, and neuroscientist A. Jean Ayres, Ph.D., likened SPD to a neurological 'traffic jam' that prevents certain parts of the brain from receiving the information needed to interpret sensory information correctly" (STAR Institute for Sensory Processing, 2025).

There are many additional ways that having SPD can impact body attunement and intuitive eating. This includes internal signals such as interoception (attunement to the signals sent by your organs), which can make it more difficult to know when you're hungry and full. Additionally, disruption of taste or smell signals can impact appetite, enjoyment of food, and even digestion.

If you have SPD or suspect you might, getting non-shaming support from professionals trained in SPD and peers who have similar lived experiences is so important.

Neurodivergence

I have some types of neurodivergence, some diagnosed and some not. It's impacted my life most by being expected to learn in the same way as neurotypical people. I struggled with shame and frustration around this for most of my life. It wasn't until I was able to learn in my bones that my value isn't tied to being like anyone else or to outward achievement that I started consistently getting curious about what works FOR ME, advocating better for my learning style and needs, and knowing I'm great just the way I am.

There are also some real advantages of my neurodivergence. I think in a very flexible way, and I can see things from a systems perspective. Everything is connected in my brain. While overwhelming at times, this allows me to see patterns, making me a good coach. My brain seeing patterns and connecting unexpected things brought me the idea for this book. I also question the norm more, and now that I'm securely attached with myself, I'm able to speak against harmful norms—loudly.

Each person is unique with different challenges and different strengths. It's so important to recognize both.

If you're neurodivergent, be sure to recognize that some of the ways intuitive eating and body attunement skills are taught may not work for you (maybe even the ways I've laid out in this book). This isn't a shortcoming of yours. You simply need a way that works for you.

Neurodivergent folks commonly experience sensory seeking and sensory avoidance. This is the body's way of supporting the nervous system and neurotransmitter regulation by managing sensory input. Keep in mind that you have sensory-*specific* needs.

When considering food or eating challenges, be curious about whether a behavior pattern may be an attempt to reduce sensory input, such as eating a narrow range of foods, soothing using food, or eating the same things over and over. If you find yourself in patterns of sensory avoidance, supporting your nervous system or regulating environmental sensory stimulation (such as reduced lighting, wearing headphones, or soft clothing) can be helpful.

Eating behaviors may also be a way to attempt to get more stimulation. It's so important not to shame yourself for this and instead get curious. What's the underlying need? You may simply need more sensory input, which you can be intentional with—choosing foods that are more sensory-rich, or making a point of getting your sensory needs met in additional ways like music, social connection, and using fidgets.

Body relationships can also be impacted by neurodivergence. If you're made to feel like there's something wrong with you by the dominant culture or it's uncomfortable to be in your body due to sensory overwhelm, it may cause you to have an adversarial relationship with your body. You may have equated feeling bad with your body being bad. It takes time to externalize that message and begin to accept yourself and trust your body's messages.

Be sure to give yourself space and time to integrate new concepts, such as the principles of Intuitive Eating and body attunement. Be creative in how you go about learning new skills. Get support from peers and professionals specifically trained in supporting neurodivergent people when you're feeling stuck. Adjust your expectations based on your capacity and your unique needs. Secure attachment will look different for you than for neurotypicals. Remember, being fed is best. Let go of judgment and eat in whatever way is most accessible for you. Beyond that, developing a nurturing relationship with food is a great goal. Know that you're amazing, just as you are.

ARFID (Avoidant/Restrictive Food Intake Disorder)

ARFID is a mental health and eating disorder recently added to the DSM-5. It's characterized by extreme food restriction that results in not meeting energy or nutrient needs. It isn't related to attempts at losing weight or body image concerns. It typically stems from fear of choking, gagging, or vomiting while eating and/or adverse sensory input from the food, such as textures, smells, etc. ARFID is more common for folks who are autistic or have anxiety, and it's correlated with sensory processing disorder (Trundle, 2025).

I mention this here because if you have an extreme aversion to eating, it's likely more than being a "picky eater" (the judgy narrative our culture tends to assign). Give yourself compassion and get support. Many providers have the approach of exposure therapy. But without safety and resourcing, this approach may set you up for more frustration and shame. I recommend reviewing the phases of trauma healing and then interviewing multiple providers who have somatic and trauma-informed care training. Attempt to find consistent support that feels deeply compassionate. Focusing on nervous system support and awareness of what's happening in your body is imperative in change and growth.

Dissociation/Disconnection

Many of the physical barriers mentioned lead to an increase in dissociation. Dissociation is on a spectrum (and I'm referring experiencing dissociation at times, not the extreme end of dissociative disorder diagnoses). If you've been diagnosed or feel that dissociation is affecting your memory or your sense of identity, causing you to disconnect from reality, or is intense or frequent, please get evaluated and professional support prior to focusing on building body attunement.

At times, people disconnect from their body when they feel unsafe. It's simply a survival strategy. And it's pretty effective! Here you are. You survived.

While dissociation helped you survive, it's limiting. And it makes body attunement really challenging. Again, please get support around this with a trained trauma-informed therapist. Learn some techniques that work well for you when you get overwhelmed by the sensations in your body to support you as you build body attunement.

One simple grounding technique I use is looking around the room (opening up your peripheral vision helps your body know you're safe) and naming five things out loud, including its color or another descriptor. For example, "I see a green plant, a soft blanket, a black fan, a white alarm clock, and a red candle." Body squeezes, holding a stuffed animal or pet, or wrapping yourself up in a blanket can also be helpful.

Next, check your self-judgment. Be sure to not think of dissociating as bad or wrong. Instead, get curious. What does this actually feel like? Numbness is a sensation too; it has discernable qualities. What's the texture, the temperature? Does it have movement or direction? Do your best to describe it.

Getting curious and increasing awareness of when and why it happens can be really helpful in supporting yourself and in discovering your underlying needs as well as what's causing you to feel unsafe.

Remember the stages of the change theory in Chapter 5: establishing safety, softening, expansion, re-establish safety, and integration. After expansion (feeling the feelings), you'll likely need to re-establish safety, which means that you may dissociate more intensely for a time after connecting to your body. This doesn't mean you're failing or not doing it right. It's your body returning to perceived safety after stepping out of your comfort zone.

If you feel as if you keep hitting your head against the wall, unable to make the progress you're hoping for, please don't assume you're flawed. It's likely just an unseen barrier(s) making you feel stuck. Barriers that can be addressed. There are so many potential barriers to body attunement, and that's good news. It's not you! The problem is one-size-fits-all cultural expectations and a lack of support.

We all need different kinds of support to thrive. Meet yourself where you're at. When change isn't happening easefully, it means you're lacking the resources you need. Return to the resourcing stage of healing. You'll be surprised by what's possible when you have what you need.

Chapter Eleven

Your Secure Attachment

When I think about what secure attachment has been for me, I have to first acknowledge that it's not a linear path with a destination. While I have literal boxes you can check in Chapter 4, that exercise isn't the best way to know if you're showing up securely attached with yourself, your body, and food.

Secure attachment doesn't feel hard like control or disconnected like avoidance. There's tension in the space between attunement/ honoring yourself and navigating real life. At first, it'll take much attention and focus, but it'll begin to feel easeful with enough practice. Secure attachment is a practice. It's not like checking off boxes or a destination. It's experiencing something new enough times that it becomes your norm, your base, and learning to carry that connection and trust with your*self,* everywhere you go.

I recently had a stressful conversation with my mom while at a partner's house. When I hung up the phone, I said to him, "I don't always eat emotionally, but when I do, it's usually about my mom. I want cookies." We had a good laugh, and he offered me brownies. I declined and asked for a hug instead; I only wanted cookies and really needed emotional support.

Later, when I got home, there was huge stack of Girl Scout cookies on my porch. I had completely forgotten that I'd ordered them. It felt like a gift from the universe. I happily ate some. Did it make me feel better? Hell yes. For a bit. And later, I talked with my therapist about my mom. Processing the emotions around the conversation with my mom made me feel a lot better, and I got clarity about my needs. All of this is secure attachment.

Secure attachment is relational. It's about feeling seen and honored. Curiosity and attunement are key. Making choices about how to care for yourself and live your life based on what feels right for you, at that moment, is the practice of relating to yourself from a place of secure attachment.

At times, this might mean doing something that seems like a bad idea or even a failure to outside appearances, like quitting a job that's sucking your soul but everyone praises you for; letting go of years of yoga practice if you're consistently getting injured or it no longer brings you joy; leaving a marriage that isn't terrible, but also not supporting you to live your fullest life; choosing to eat meat again if you've been vegetarian or vegan but it feels like restriction; breaking up with diets; or saying no to a big opportunity that'll stretch you too thin.

Secure attachment is all about tuning in to your body, your heart, and making decisions based on who and where you are in this moment while also looking out for future you when you're resourced to do so. Secure attachment looks like loving yourself in all your struggles and joys, in a beautiful, nurturing relationship. Secure attachment with yourself means showing up for you, no matter what.

There's no way for someone to look at you or your actions and know for sure if you're acting from a place of secure attachment.

> *Only you can know what feels right.*

For me, it feels soft and fierce all at once. Deeply intimate, yet playful. I love feeling seen and honoring myself.

A dear client who has done this work shared what secure attachment with themselves, food, and their body means to them.

"In one word, secure attachment with myself, food, and my body means trust. Trusting my body's signals. Trusting my mind to listen to and act on those signals. Trusting the process of rejecting diet culture and embracing the anger, grief, freedom, and ease that comes with it. Trusting my choices, whether with food, movement, activities and experiences, even trusting when the choice is a hard nope. Trusting that I'm on the right path for me, for only me, no one else. Trusting that I've got my own back.

This isn't to say building trust with oneself—with myself—is easy. In fact, it can be downright painful to quiet the chatter saying I'm not good enough, that how I am in the world is wrong or bad, that I don't fit here. But when I show up for myself time and time again, when I feel ease and peace and acceptance when I look at myself in the mirror, when I can feel in my bones this journey toward freedom was meant for me— that's all the evidence I need that I've built a relationship with myself, food, and my body rooted in trust, nurtured by trust, alive with trust."

—BM, a beautiful client

The unconditional nature of secure attachment is like a bedrock that you can rely on in the best of times and the worst of times. Imagine if you really saw all of yourself, without judgment, if you could trust yourself to provide wisdom, guidance, love, nurturance, and the complete acceptance you deserve. Imagine if you had your own back, unconditionally.

- What would you do differently?
- What would the voices inside your head sound like?
- What would you tell yourself?
- What would you need to hear?
- What would you need to hear over and over again?
- How would you show up for yourself?
- What would you need to feel or experience?
- What would make you feel seen, heard, and cared for?
- How often are you saying or giving yourself those things?
- Is it often enough?

That's the distance between where you are now and secure attachment. I hope this book brought you a little closer. You've got this. You deserve it.

You are
already
enough.

Appendix A

My Story

I went on my first diet at around age 10. I thought my body was too big and had thought so for as long as I can remember. I don't know exactly where those thoughts came from. There wasn't one big shaming event. I don't think my parents said much about my body. I know I was comparing myself to my classmates and felt much bigger than most of the other girls, even though I was the youngest in my class. I saw my mom dieting and thought it was the thing to do. Besides, the brightly colored macro tracking cards, the "free foods," like plain popcorn or sugar-free Jello, and sweating to the oldies with Richard Simmons sounded fun. I also felt like it was something my mom and I could do together, like it would bring us more connection. It didn't bring real connection, only conditional attention and praise.

> *It's not your fault.*

At 13 years old, I went to visit my grandparents in Wisconsin for the summer. My grandmother always had sugary cereal (whatever we asked for), soda, snacks, and fresh homemade cookies in the

179

cookie jar. We ate large family meals and had ice cream cones on the porch at night. My grandparents would even make me fancy drinks—one of my favorites was lemon lime soda with crushed pineapple and maraschino cherries on top. I loved it! It felt fun and exciting to have so many options. I especially loved having permission to eat so many treats. Having unfettered access to all those treats was new for me, and I spent a lot of time thinking about food. But still, I wanted to eat more than I thought I "should," so I snuck food. I remember eating the maraschino cherries and drinking the juice straight from the jar when no one was home. Now I know I can have cherries whenever I want, no need to sneak around.

I probably gained 20 pounds that summer, and when I got home, I could tell my mom was worried about the weight gain. When she saw me, she had a look of shock on her face. She asked me how much I'd gained and asked, "What have you been eating?!" The heat rose in my cheeks, and I tried to hide by wrapping my arms across my belly. I remember beating myself up about eating so much.

So, the dieting continued. What I didn't know then, and neither did my mother, is that it's completely natural (and important!) for young women to gain weight (sources are all over the board but cite between 15-50 pounds between 10-16 years old as a normal part of puberty).

For a few years, as a teenager, food took a back burner when I discovered smoking, drugs, and alcohol. I felt better when I was high or drunk and used substances to check out. Then I discovered stimulants, starting with high doses of no-doze caffeine pills and graduating to crank and even meth (when I could get my hands on it). I used all day, every day. It made life feel more bearable. I liked that they helped me feel productive and loved the bonus effect of taking away my appetite.

I lost so much weight.

People were commenting on my body, saying how great I looked.

It's so gross to me now—that people were congratulating me for being thin when it was the result of a serious drug addiction. I liked the attention at first, but it also added to me feeling scrutinized. It felt like I had to keep it up; the praise and attention were conditional. It was clear that looking a certain way (thin) gained me more acceptance and love. Eventually, I lost "too much." It was much less noticeable with clothes on, but I was so thin that it was becoming impossible to hide. If you saw me naked, you could count my ribs from across the room. My mom got worried when she hugged me one day and could feel how frail I'd become. She commented about how my shoulder blades jutted out. A girlfriend told me I looked like an anorexic cow. Boyfriends told me I was getting way too thin. That didn't stop me; I thought being that thin was a good thing. I finally felt some relief from my body hatred. But I was still filled with shame. I still didn't feel good enough because of who I was, the shame I held, and my body. There were still parts of my body that I disliked, parts I tried to hide.

At 17, I hit a wall with my drug use. Fortunately, I had the privileges of relatively supportive parents and access to treatment for my substance abuse paid for by our family health insurance. I went through treatment and began my recovery journey. I gained about 25 pounds—which my body needed but made me very uncomfortable. It definitely tempted me to go back to using drugs.

> *You are not broken.*

I got pregnant almost immediately after treatment and gained a bunch of weight with my pregnancy. The doctor told me I needed to "slow down" on weight gain. I worried about it, but ultimately, I couldn't control my appetite. After my daughter was born, I mostly ate pretzels. They were low-calorie. I wanted to lose the "pregnancy weight" as soon as possible, but I was still breastfeeding, and I didn't think I could manage a full-blown diet. When my daughter was a year old, I did slim down quickly, only having two diet protein shakes and a Lean Cuisine in a day. I got back into my pre-pregnancy jeans. But my body had completely changed, so I still wasn't happy. I'd curse my body for how it looked in my favorite old jeans. I was caught back up in the restrict, binge, shame cycle that had started at 10 years old.

I dieted off and on for over 20 years, caught in the endless hamster wheel of restricting food, then bingeing, followed by hating myself—what I've come to know as the cycle of dieting. I always felt better when I had a plan to lose weight or "get in shape." That feeling sucked me in, bringing me some relief from the feeling that I wasn't good enough or that there was something wrong with me. As long as I was seeking thinness, trying to control or manage my body and my appetite, I felt almost acceptable and in control.

The dieting cycle always started with feeling like I needed a change because there was something wrong—something wrong with my body or the way I ate, or sometimes even just feeling depressed or anxious about life. Most often, it was my body, and anything could trigger feeling bad about my body—an upcoming event, having to wear a bathing suit, being around thin friends or friends talking about losing weight, how I looked in a picture, shopping for clothes, the number on the scale, being winded, going to the doctor, other people in recovery saying they're cutting out sugar, digestive issues, or any other health issue.

Whatever the reason, I'd decide that I needed to go on the latest fad diet, starting Monday. I'd spend the rest of the week and weekend eating. Intuitive Eating calls this Last Supper eating. I'd eat and eat in anticipation of the impending restriction. I'd make a point of getting foods like pizza, cake, ice cream, and my favorite takeout—foods I knew were banned on the diet. I'd eat up all the foods in the house I thought of as "junk" so I wouldn't be tempted to eat them on the diet. I'd spend the weekend prepping. I'd look up recipes, fill the house with the required foods, and chop so many veggies. It felt a bit exciting, and I felt good knowing I had a "plan of attack."

Oftentimes, I'd follow the diet perfectly for months, since that's my personality type, or maybe just anxious attachment. And it worked! Or so I thought. I'd lose weight, sure, but the loss was always temporary. Eventually, some event like a holiday, vacation, or celebration would come up, and I'd decide to break the diet. I'd binge all the foods that had been off limits. I'd eat so much, knowing the next diet was just around the corner.

Over time, I'd always gain the weight back. I'd feel so much shame about my perceived lack of willpower, bingeing, and my body. I thought it was my fault. I didn't know diets don't work (the 2-year failure rate is 95% (Chastain, 2025). Diets only set us up for more shame. If you want to read more about why diets don't work, check out Appendix B.

I spent most of my twenties obsessed with food. If there was a cake in the house, I couldn't walk past the kitchen without stopping to sneak bites. At times, I'd wolf down treats while sitting in my car in the grocery store parking lot or hide wrappers so no one would know how much I'd eaten. When I wasn't on a diet, I'd find myself "numbing" with food most nights while watching TV after the kids went to bed. I would start with some chips, then get ice cream or candy or cookies or cake, and I'd often finish off the whole bag or box. Even when I was on diets, I'd usually find some food that was "allowed" or "free" to binge on, like low-fat cookies, veggies like cucumbers or celery, air-popped popcorn sprayed with I Can't Believe It's Not Butter!, or rice cakes.

At 26, I became a Registered Nurse. I loved helping people and was good at my job. I thought I was learning a lot about health, but now I see that I was learning just as much about weight stigma and anti-fat bias as health. I remember the comments about people being "overweight" because of their choices, the shaming they received simply for looking a certain way from doctors and other nurses. I see now that being in that environment added to my own negative body image and disordered eating. I started wanting to be "healthier" in addition to wanting to be thin. This translated into more attempts at "clean eating" and exercising harder.

I tended toward overworking, and after a few years, I injured my back. The pain was terrible. I could no longer lift patients and was devastated to have to stop working at the bedside. I got a super stressful desk job doing case management. Overworking and perfectionism seeped in more and more. I started having some serious health issues and was told by naturopaths that I needed to change my diet to heal. This meant more and more restrictive diets. I tried paleo, fasting, and cutting out gluten, dairy, legumes, sugar, grains, and even many fruits and veggies. I did the low FODMAP + Specific Carbohydrate Diet. I did the Whole30 four times. A friend asked why I didn't just stay on Whole30 forever. Despite how skewed my thinking was, never eating a piece of cake again didn't seem right.

On these diets, I'd often binge foods that were "allowed," like dried mango, cashew butter and bananas, sweet potato, or whatever had some carbs or fat. And when I'd go off the diet, I'd feel like shit. I'd binge and beat myself up. I thought it was a physical reaction to bingeing or eating foods that weren't allowed, but now I know much of that bad feeling was an emotional shame storm raging in my body.

I thought my health problems were my fault and that if only I could just continue eating perfectly, I'd be cured. Many foods seemed to trigger symptoms like bloating, joint pain, constipation or diarrhea, and headaches. When I'd go off the diet or binge any foods, even the ones I considered healthy, those symptoms would be so bad that I thought for sure it had to be the foods I was eating. I was scared to eat beyond my narrow window of foods I thought were safe. At the same time, I felt desperate to eat more and craved the foods I was afraid of. I can see now that I had disordered eating most of my life, and it had progressed to a full-blown eating disorder: orthorexia. I also know now that the stress of restricting and my fear of food added significantly to my digestive problems.

At that point, in addition to being a nurse and being in long-term recovery from alcohol and substance use disorder, I'd gone through training to become an Integrative Nurse Coach. I started my own side business, coaching people in self-care, health, and wellness. While I loved the work, I felt so much shame. I thought if people knew what a shitshow my relationship was with food, they'd know I was a fraud.

I was in a constant battle with food, my body, and my hunger. The worst part was that I didn't trust myself. I didn't think I COULD be trusted. I thought there was something wrong with me.

I was exhausted and had tried everything.

At some point, I even tried eating whatever I wanted, and I just ate and ate. I remember bingeing on a huge bowl of Halloween candy, thinking there had to be a stopping point, but I sure didn't find it. I'd even eat some kind of palette cleanser like York Peppermint Patties so I could enjoy the other candy again after my mouth started feeling too gross. So, I thought that experiment with eating whatever I wanted had failed too. I didn't want to just give up on my health, but I didn't think I could go on like this.

I thought the only way to change was to control and manage food and my body better—to do it HARDER.

> *It's not your fault.*
> *You are not broken.*

Healing

One day, I was measuring my broccoli, and the absurdity of having to measure BROCCOLI hit me. I woke up, realizing I'd been stuck in this pattern of restriction/bingeing and self-hatred for decades. I saw that even with all of my knowledge, my education and training, and all of my efforts, this approach simply wasn't working. I finally saw that it was never going to work if I kept doing the same thing.

I needed help, and I was lucky enough to find an Intuitive Eating-trained therapist (Hilary from The Center for Body Trust— thank you so much!). She asked me about the last time I had a deeply satisfying meal. I was floored. No one had ever asked me about my food *satisfaction*. I was IN.

As I learned about the principles of Intuitive Eating, I knew this was what I'd needed all along. It included ME and didn't solely focus on food. It was so different than anything I'd tried before, but I wasn't sure I could learn to trust myself.

There was a huge learning curve. It was painful to let go of "shoulds" when rules about what is and isn't "healthy" had been the way I made decisions about what to eat for YEARS. I also had to navigate some tricky areas around my health and food sensitivities. I found it difficult to find resources with nuance in the Intuitive

Eating literature. And, honestly, I was worried about gaining weight, but ultimately, I found freedom. I healed my relationship with food and my body.

> *My body houses my soul.*
> *My purpose is to satisfy my soul.*

Recently, a dear client said she wanted to make friends with food and make friends with her body. That's what it was like for me. I was finally able to stop fighting my body. I worked to cultivate a friendship with it. Food became nourishment and something I could enjoy. It too, became my friend.

For the first time in my life, food felt right-sized. When I got hungry, I made eating a priority. I paid attention to feeling full. I didn't always stop there, but most of the time I did. When I kept eating, it was a conscious choice. I found satisfaction and peace.

I remember my astonishment when I declined some cupcakes at a kid's birthday party because I simply didn't want any, or when I stopped eating my pasta, even though it tasted incredible, just because I was full. I knew I could have more at any time. At Thanksgiving, I took only the foods I actually wanted, and I didn't eat until I felt sick. Craving veggies or noticing my body getting antsy when I needed to move my bones was also surprising and awesome. I learned to make decisions with discernment (based on what my body wanted and needed) and the empowerment of living from a place of choice rather than "shoulds."

I went to Europe for the first time at the beginning of eating intuitively. Feeling free to have the experience of trying all the foods I wanted was so incredible. In Bruges, Belgium, I ate more chocolates than I usually did. They were delicious. I really got to enjoy them. But I also tuned in to my body and noticed how I felt after eating them. When I ate several at a time, it didn't feel great physically and after a few days, they lost their shininess.

I remember going into a cheese shop. To my delight, they were also a catering company. They had a large case of gourmet appetizers to sample. The salesperson helped me pick by telling me his favorites and describing the flavors. He carefully heated and plated each morsel. It felt indulgent and magical. Suddenly, I understood foodies in a way I never had before.

My favorite meal was in a restaurant on the ground floor of a hostel. They had a patio in the back with party lights strung just right, twinkling in the night. Lovely music poured out to the patio. The temperature outside, the company, the atmosphere all felt so good. I asked the server what she liked, and she suggested the Dover sole (it was fresh, of course). I do like fish, but I typically reserved it to be a "healthy" dish that I "should" eat when I cooked at home. I would never have ordered the fish unless I was on a diet. But it sounded yummy, so I took a chance. She was so right. It was delicious. It turns out that butter is a critical ingredient in white fish dishes. All of those years of trying to make myself eat healthy had been *ruining my fish experience*. Who knew that my favorite meal on a ten-day trip in Europe could be FISH? When I was mired in the restrict/binge cycle, I would've gone on vacation binge mode. I would've ordered the things that were "off-limits" and stuffed myself at every opportunity (and beat myself up after). I would've missed the pleasure of trying something new. I can still feel the energy, taste the food, hear the music. The entire experience deeply satisfied me.

It was so awesome to just enjoy food without guilt or a plan to "get back on track." But healing was more than that. I learned to listen to my body, I learned to trust it, and most importantly, my body learned to trust me. My body had to feel safe and trust that I'd feed it, care for it, and listen to it.

I realized that to fully heal, I needed to repair all the years of damage to the relationship with my body.

My body is my home, my ally, not my enemy.

As soon as I was solid in my personal practice of intuitive eating, I decided to get certified and shift the focus of my coaching practice. I realized that nearly everyone I knew was struggling under the weight of diet culture. I knew so many people would benefit from this work and it became my life passion.

Working with my clients brought me so much joy. It also supported my own growth. I loved this work so much that it motivated me to become as effective as possible, seeking out as much education, training, and information as I could consume.

The universe works in mysterious ways. One day, I got a call from my friend Cassie, who had previously worked as my assistant. She had become a business coach and was supporting clients with their businesses. She told me that she regularly used things I taught her about growth and change to support her clients. She said that my methods didn't solely apply to intuitive eating, and she thought I should create my own model. I felt so flattered but wasn't sure what the foundation of my model would be.

That call came in about six months before I listened to *Poly-Secure* and had the realization that attachment theory also applies to our relationship with food and body. When I discovered that it wasn't really being applied in this way, I knew that I wanted to develop the idea further.

And so, the food and body attachment model was born! Thank you, Cassie, for seeing something in me I couldn't yet see.

This is the model I wish I'd had when I was struggling. I'm so honored to get to share it with you!

Happily Ever After

The process of creating the food and body attachment model supported an even deeper level of healing in me. My foundation of self-trust has grown wider and deeper. I no longer blame myself when my body hurts or life isn't going the way I'd hoped. I understand how to process my feelings, discover my needs, and honor my body. And when I don't know how, I get support. I practice compassion and curiosity with myself. I'm on my body's team.

The romantic relationship I set out to save didn't work out. In the past, that would've been the happily ever after I was looking for. Now I seek my happily ever after in my relationship with myself. I'm true to myself. I learned that far too often, I do more than my fair share of work in relationships. I now choose relationships that meet me in the middle, relationships where I feel seen, cared for, and secure. Relationships that reflect and amplify the beautiful relationship I have with myself.

Today, I'm learning how to satisfy my soul. I rest, I play, I dance, I kiss, I eat. My work and writing are a huge part of my soul satisfaction. Thank you for being here with me.

We are already enough.

Diets Don't Work

You're here for a reason. Either you tried dieting but it didn't work, you've seen others try to diet and the mess it caused them, or you don't want to diet. Trust your lived experience. Here are some specific resources to dive into if you find that you have a lingering desire to diet or the idea that they might work is still loud in your head.

Try this exercise. Get a piece of paper and turn it horizontally. Draw a line with hash marks from one to your current age. Mark all the ages you attempted diets. Then mark the times when you felt you should diet or restrict in some way. For each of those marks, what was your general feeling about yourself before? How did you feel after? Did you lose weight? If so, how long did it take to gain it back? Did you gain more than you lost?

So often we don't look at the impact of a diet. We think, "It worked, until…" without ever considering the harm. Dieting/restricting or trying to control or manage food and your body that leads to short-term weight loss is not successful. If a medication only worked for a short time, and caused a bunch of negative side effects, it would never be approved by the FDA. Why do we feel it's okay for ineffective and harmful diets to regularly be recommended by doctors?

Why Diets Don't Work

You start out feeling like crap about yourself. Shame isn't effective for long-term, sustainable change. Additionally, you can't shame yourself into loving, accepting, or feeling good about yourself.

So, you feel bad about yourself and decide that losing weight is the solution to feeling bad (spoiler, it's not). You choose a diet and get excited. You might even calculate out how long it'll take you to reach your goals. *If I start on Monday, it'll take x weeks.* You dream about all the love, acceptance, and joy you'll feel once you've reached the goal. You might tell people your dieting plans or join groups who congratulate you for being a "good fatty" and trying to lose weight, no matter the methods or cost. "No pain, no gain," right?

You start a diet or restricting in some new way. While restricting, your body thinks it's in a famine. So, it's going to begin resisting weight loss from day one. Your hunger signals go up. Your fullness signals go down. You become increasingly preoccupied with food. Eventually, your (very reasonable) hunger will drive you to go off the diet, maybe the first day, maybe after years of restricting.

While dieting/restricting, your body will slow your metabolism so you don't burn through your food as quickly. You lose muscle mass. When you go back to eating more than you did while dieting, your body will metabolize it differently and attempt to store fat to make you more resilient during the next "famine." You gain weight.[36]

When you go off the diet, you'll feel like crap about yourself again for being a "failure." That's dysregulating to your nervous system and creates an emotional storm. In addition to all your body signals making you want to eat to resist the perceived famine, you'll be prone to soothe your nervous system and stormy emotions using food.

---

36. One of my clients told me that when she hears a friend mention a diet she says, "Oh, you mean weight cycling?" That's EXACTLY what diets lead to. I love her so much.

You likely believe the diet worked until you lost your willpower. This narrative keeps you thinking you're a failure, there's something wrong with you, you can't trust yourself, and you need to keep trying diets until you finally succeed. The truth is diets stop "working" when *you can no longer resist your biological needs. In other words, they don't work.*

If you're trying to lose weight to feel accepted, sexy, or desired, it doesn't work because it keeps you feeling like there's something wrong with you. The acceptance you seek is conditional and short-lived; you get compliments when you're thinner. When you gain the weight back, you stop getting compliments. This cycle adds to feeling like there's something wrong with you as you are. This all adds to the attachment wounds and trauma you have.

If you're trying to lose weight for your health, diets don't work because they add to the allostatic load (overall stress and inflammation in your body). They screw up your hunger and fullness hormones, your metabolism, your gut, and stress hormones. Diets also lead to weight cycling, which is worse for your body than just being at a higher but steady weight.

Dieting and restricting also distract from what you really need to be healthy. For example, sleep is so important for overall health. If you go to bed hungry, you're less likely to get quality sleep. If you're getting up early to fit in your rigid workout routine, you might be burning the candles at both ends. This stresses your whole system and increases your appetite. The ends don't justify the means.

Answer the following question the best you can:
- What do I think I want by dieting/restricting or losing weight?

For each desire, list out possible underlying desires.
- What are some non-diet ways you might meet your underlying needs?

For example:

What I think my desires might be:
I want to be healthy.

Possible underlying desires:
I want...
more energy
to feel different (better)
to be less afraid of illness or death
to feel confident I'm taking care of myself
to make others in my life happy

Next, list ways you might meet those underlying desires without focusing on weight. For example:

Non-diet ways I might meet these desires:
I can...
develop a movement practice
add in more foods that make me feel good
get better sleep
face fears of death
take care of my health conditions through non-diet measures (like eating more fiber and taking fish oil for improving cholesterol)

Here's a litmus test to see if your desire is truly what you think it is or if there's diet culture lurking below the surface. Are you doing everything you can (other than dieting) to support your underlying needs and desires? If not, your motive to diet might be more about appearance and anti-fat bias. For example, if you say you want to be healthy but aren't willing to prioritize sleep, you're likely more concerned about weight loss for aesthetic reasons than you might want to admit.

> *Ask yourself, why do you want to weigh less or look a certain way?*

Is it because you face weight stigma?

This is a valid concern. Only you can decide if it's worth it to try to make your body smaller to experience less stigma. But please consider if there are ways you might find more acceptance and love as you are. So much of the anti-diet messaging is about individual actions you can take, but we all need love and community. Consider joining fat-positive groups in your community and online.

A recent study shows that rather than changing your body to avoid being fat, "opting in" to the identity of fat and finding belonging in the fat community improves body image. Resisting the messaging of weight stigma is associated with better outcomes than internalization of those messages (Meadows & Higgs, 2022).

Build relationships with people who understand weight stigma and love you as you are. Take a hard look at the relationships, communities, and spaces you're regularly in. Do you feel safe, welcome, and considered in them? If not, can you deprioritize or even leave these relationships or spaces entirely? It can be painful to let go of people and communities, but in the end, it can be best for your well-being. Letting go of people and communities that don't support you can make space for those that will.

Is it because a caregiver or loved one told you that no one would love you or want to marry you unless you lost weight?

If they did, first off, I'm so sorry. Not only is that not true, but it's so harmful. You deserved better. SO, I want you to give yourself better... no more internalizing harmful messages that you aren't lovable or enough as you are. Losing weight to be loved is conditional and won't last. And don't you want people to love you for you and not for how you look? That's the kind of love that lasts through illness, aging, and the cycles of life.

Is it because you believe you need to look a specific way for your gender?

While everyone is impacted by gender stereotypes, I wanted to bring particular attention to the ways queer people are impacted on a deeper level. Gender and sexual minorities have a 2-4x higher rate of eating disorders than their cis-heterosexual counterparts. When discrimination[37] is experienced, the rate of eating disorders increases even more (Kamody, 2020).

Wanting to lose weight to appear more like the stereotypes of your gender can be due to many needs—wanting to be safe, seen, or desired, to name a few. These are completely valid needs. I recommend the book *Belly of the Beast* by Da'Shaun L. Harrison and their exploration of desirability politics, a function of systems of oppression that award people considered desirable (thin, white, straight, cis-gendered) more autonomy and privilege and harm those deemed undesirable.

Only you can decide what is the best way to reach for your needs to be met. My hope is the questions below will help you explore the influence of stereotypes and desirability politics on your gender expression.

- What is the potential cost to you of pursing weight loss?
- How is our culture's binary and narrow view of gender influencing the way you feel you need to look to affirm your gender?
- Are you trying to meet stereotypes, perceived requirements, expectations, or "shoulds" about your gender, or are you trying to feel more authentic to yourself?

---

37. The study says, "perceived discrimination," but I prefer to just say discrimination. Those of us who have been marginalized know when we've been discriminated against.

◈ What needs do you have around your gender? What are non-diet ways that might support those needs?

There are so many reasons you might want to lose weight. Life is easier in a lot of ways when you're thinner, but that doesn't mean it's right for you to have to contort yourself to have the same freedoms and privileges as others. Look deeply at your needs, desires, and motives; you might be surprised to find that dieting is preventing you from much of the peace and self-acceptance that would be deeply nourishing.

I know these exercises can be heavy. The heaviness and grief that might come up is part of why you might be tempted to just try another diet. Dieting allows you to avoid these deeper feelings and pain, temporarily. But over the long haul, dieting makes it worse. It'll never give you the deepest things you desire.

When we zoom out and look at all the evidence, diets don't work, and ultimately, they undermine your overall health and wellbeing in deeply important ways.

For more information, here are some links to great organizations that highlight the science showing diets don't work:

◈ asdah.org/haes
◈ haeshealthsheets.com/
   why-we-dont-recommend-intentional-weight-loss
◈ intuitiveeating.org/studies
◈ weightandhealthcare.substack.com/p/the-research-post
◈ weightinclusivemedicine.org/learn

Enough.

Acknowledgments

S o many people supported this book's creation and supported me personally while writing it. First, Jessica Fern, whose books have deeply supported my relational growth, and who was my inspiration in creating the food and body attachment model. Thank you for taking the time to encourage me and help me hash out the idea.

To the people who influenced me with your work; who have written books, created podcasts, offered trainings, posted your thoughts on social media, and put your energy into making the world a better place. You planted seeds, provided soft landings, and helped me be a better coach. You showed me the areas of growth I needed to focus on to be who I want to be in the world. Every bit of your invaluable resources added to this book.

To my coaches, Amy Isaman and River Kai; my editor Kayla Vokolek and unofficial editor Katherine Kozioziemski; my VA Brooke; Rachel Kuhn my indexer; and Domini Dragoone, my cover artist and book designer, thank you for holding my hand through this process. I couldn't have done it without you.

To Angel Austin, my sensitivity reader, thank you for believing in my desire to make this book accessible and helpful to as many people as possible. Thank you for speaking truthfully, for your vulnerability, candor, and care in guiding me. This book is better because of you.

To all my clients, holy shit, y'all are the best. Thank you for your trust, your vulnerability, your patience with my graphics, and for teaching me as much as or more than I taught you. Our work together helped me learn, see patterns, understand our shared humanity so much more, and to develop this model.

To my colleagues who encouraged me and who roll up their sleeves every day to help clients and one another grow in this work. To my daughter, who I love more than words, and who endlessly inspires me to grow. To all my friends and chosen family, you put up with me talking about publishing a book for 4+ years and were my cheerleaders when I didn't know how it was going to happen. Y'all help me remember I'm already enough.

Additional Resources

Attachment Theory
- **The Secure Relationship:** thesecurerelationship.com

BMI Is Bogus
- **Helpful NPR article:** npr.org/2009/07/04/106268439/top-10-reasons-why-the-bmi-is-bogus
- **Ragen Chastain's blog:** weightandhealthcare.substack.com/p/whats-the-problem-with-bmi-and-how

Emotional Sovereignty School
- **Learn how to process your emotions:** centerforemotionaleducation.com/emotional-sovereignty-school

The Fat Spectrum aka Fategories
- **Linda of *Fluffy Kitten Party* blog:** fluffykittenparty.com/2021/06/01/fategories-understanding-smallfat-fragility-the-fat-spectrum
- **Ash of *The Fat Lip* podcast and blog:** thefatlip.com/2016/12/20/beyond-superfat-rethinking-the-farthest-end-of-the-fat-spectrum

Intuitive Eating

- The official Intuitive Eating website, including the 10 Principles of Intuitive Eating and a directory of Certified Intuitive Eating Professionals: intuitiveeating.org

Instagram

Too many to list here. It's so important to see a wide variety of bodies represented. If you're on social media, consider unfollowing accounts where the white thin ideal is centered or any accounts that make you feel bad when you see their content. For some great size-inclusive accounts, consider going to my Instagram and checking out who I follow. **@coachtiffanyrn**

Podcasts

- *The Anti-Diet Life* by Leah Hortin
- *AuDHD Flourishing* by Mattia Maurée
- *Body Liberation for All* by Dalia Kinsey, RD, LD
- *The Body Trust* podcast by Dana Sturtevant, Hilary Kinavey, and Sirius Bonner
- *Food Psych* by Christy Harrison
- *HAES® Pod: The Official Health at Every Size® Podcast* by ASDAH
- *How to Survive the End of the World* by Autumn Brown and adrienne maree brown
- *The Live Your Best Fat Life Podcast* by Tiana Dodson
- *Maintenance Phase* by Aubrey Gordon & Michael Hobbes
- *Recovery Bites* by Karin Lewis, MA, LMFT, CEDS (a bit more science/academic)
- *The Space Beyond Scarce* by Kate Holly
- *This Is (Not) About Your Body* by Jessi Kneeland
- *Unsolicited: Fatties Talk Back* by Marquisele Mercedes, Da'Shaun Harrison, Caleb Luna, Bryan Guffey, and Jordan Underwood

- *Weight For It* by Ronald Young Jr
- *Your Two-Spirit Aunties* by Shilo George and Brianna Bragg

Recovery Resources

- **Love Sober:** www.lovesober.com
- **SHE RECOVERS®:** sherecovers.org
- **Soberful:** soberful.com

Size-Inclusive Healthcare, Support, and Fat Advocacy

- **Asher Larmie:** www.fatdoctor.co.uk
- **Association for Size Diversity and Health: Health at Every Size®:** asdah.org
- **Association for Weight and Size Inclusive Medicine:** weightinclusivemedicine.org/learn
- *Fat Self-Care* **Substack by Anna Louise Eileen Chapman: "Open Letter to Brené Brown":** fatselfcare.substack.com/p/an-open-letter-i-wrote-to-brene-brown
- **National Association to Advance Fat Acceptance:** naafa.org
- **Ragen Chastain's Substack:** weightandhealthcare.substack.com
- **Shilo George:** shilogeorge.com

Videos

- **Coach Tiffany:** *Landing Exercise.* youtube.com/watch?v=uifegj1ut-Y
- **Marilyn Wann:** *Fighting Fat Fear. UCLA.* youtube.com/watch?v=_g8-QWDqTdM

A Few of the Books
I Recommend

- *Anti-Diet* by Christy Harrison, MPH, RD
- *Belly of the Beast* by Da'Shaun L. Harrison
- *Black Disability Politics* by Sami Schalk, PhD
- *The Body is Not an Apology* by Sonya Renee Taylor
- *Body Neutral* by Jessi Kneeland
- *Burnout* by Emily Nagoski, PhD & Amelia Nagoski, DMA
- *Caste* by Isabel Wilkerson
- *Decolonizing Wellness* by Dalia Kinsey, RD, LD
- *Emergent Strategy* by adrienne maree brown
- *Fearing the Black Body* by Sabrina Strings, PhD
- *Food Isn't Medicine* by Dr. Joshua Wolrich
- *Good Inside* by Dr. Becky Kennedy
- *I Thought It Was Just Me (But It Isn't)* by Brené Brown, PhD, LMSW
- *Intuitive Eating, 4th Edition* by Evelyn Tribole, MS, RDN and Elyse Resch, MS, RDN
- *It's Always Been Ours* by Jessica Wilson, MS, RD
- *My Grandmother's Hands* by Resmaa Menakem, MSW, LICSW, SEP
- *Pleasure Activism* by adrienne maree brown

- *Polysecure* by Jessica Fern, MS
- *Polywise* by Jessica Fern, MS & David Cooley
- *Reclaiming Body Trust* by Hilary Kinavey, MS, LPC and Dana Sturtevant, MS, RD
- *Rest Is Resistance* by Tricia Hersey
- *Self-Compassion* by Kristin Neff, PhD
- *Unmasking Autism* by Devon Price, PhD
- *Weightless* by Evette Dionne
- *What it Takes to Heal* by Prentis Hemphill
- *What We Don't Talk About When We Talk About Fat* by Aubrey Gordon
- *You Are Your Best Thing* by Tarana Burke and Brené Brown, PhD, LMSW
- *"You Just Need to Lose Weight"* by Aubrey Gordon

Index

References

Additude Mag. (2025, May 9). *What is Sensory Processing Disorder.* Retrieved from Additude Mag: https://www.additudemag.com/ what-is-sensory-processing-disorder

Brown, T. B. (2022). *You Are Your Best Thing: Vulnerablity, Shame Resilience, and The Black Experience.* New York: Random House .

Butterfly Foundation. (2025, May 9). *Drugs, Alcohol, and Eating Disorders.* Retrieved from National Eating Disorders Collaboration: https://nedc.com.au/eating-disorder-resources/find-resources/ show/issue-58-i-the-link-between-drugs-alcohol-and-eating-disorders

Chastain, R. (2025, May 21). *Who Says Dieting Fails Most of Time.* Retrieved from Weight and Healthcare substack: https://weightandhealthcare.substack.com/p/who-says-dieting-fails-the-majority

Dionne, E. (2022). *Weightless: Making Space for my Resilient Body and Soul.* New York: Ecco.

Embodied Recovery for Eating Disorders. (2020). Four Princilples of ERED. North Carolina.

Equity in the Center. (2025, May 9). *Racial Equity Tools Glossary.* Retrieved from Racial Equity Tools: https://www.racialequity-tools.org/glossary

Gerhardt, L. (2025, May 10). *Fategories – Understanding the Fat Spectrum.* Retrieved from Fluffy Kitten Party: https://fluffy-kittenparty.com/2021/06/01/fategories-understanding-small-fat-fragility-the-fat-spectrum

Gordon, A. (2020). *What We Don't Talk About When We Talk About Fat.* Boston: Beacon Press.

Harrison, C. (2025, May 9). *What is Diet Culture.* Retrieved from Christy Harrision: https://christyharrison.com/blog/what-is-diet-culture

Harvard College. (2024, Jan 10). *Systems of Oppression.* Retrieved from Havard Global Health Institute: https://globalhealth.harvard.edu/domains/systems-of-oppression

Kamody, R. C. (2020). Disparities in DSM-5 defined eating disorders by sexual orientation among U.S. adults. *The International journal of eating disorders,* 53(2), 278–287. doi:https://doi.org/10.1002/eat.23193

Meadows, A., & Higgs, S. (2022, Sept 1). Challenging oppression: A social identity model of stigma resistance in higher-weight individuals. *Science Direct, Body Image, 42,* pp. 237-245. doi:https://doi.org/10.1016/j.bodyim.2022.06.004

MindOnly. (2025, May 9). *John Bowlby and Attachment Theory.* Retrieved from The Attachment Project: https://www.attachmentproject.com/attachment-theory/john-bowlby/

Nagoski, E., & Nagoski, A. (2019). *Burnout: The Secret to Unlocking the Stress Cycle.* New York: Ballantine Books.

National Eating Disorders Association. (2025, May 9). *What is Orthorexia?* Retrieved from National Eating Disorders Association: https://www.nationaleatingdisorders.org/orthorexia

Northville, F. (2025, May 21). *Can You Have High Cholestorol if You Are Underweight?* Retrieved from Eating Disorder Resources: https://eatingdisorderresources.com/can-you-have-high-cholesterol-if-you-are-underweight/#Does_starvation_cause_high_cholesterol

Resch, E., & Tribole, E. (2020). *Intuitive Eating: A Revolutionary Program That Works .* New York: St. Martin's Press.

Resch, E., & Tribole, E. (2025, May 9). *The Original Intuitive Eating Pros*. Retrieved from 10 Principles of Intuitive Eating: https://www.intuitiveeating.org/about-us/10-principles-of-intuitive-eating

STAR Institute for Sensory Processing. (2025, June 12). *About us*. Retrieved from Sensoryhealth.org: https://sensoryhealth.org/basic/about-us

STAR Institute for Sensory Processing. (2025, May 9). *Understanding the Sensory Integration Process*. Retrieved from Sensory Health: https://sensoryhealth.org/basic/understanding-sensory-processing-disorder

Strings, S. (2019). In S. Strings, *Fearing the Black Body: The Racial Origins of Fat Phobia*. New York: New York University Press.

Tribole, E. (2025, May 9). *Definition of Intuitive Eating*. Retrieved from Intuitive Eating: https://www.intuitiveeating.org/definition-of-intuitive-eating

Tribole, E. M., & Resch, E. (2025, June 6). *10 Principles of Intuitive Eating*. Retrieved from Intuitiveeating.org: https://www.intuitiveeating.org/about-us/10-principles-of-intuitive-eating

Trundle, H. (2025, May 9). *ARFID and Sensory Processing Issues*. Retrieved from Integrated Eating: https://www.integratedeating.com/blog/2021/5/10/arfid-and-sensory-processing-issues

U.S. Dept of Agriculture. (2025, May 21). *Food Security in the U.S. - Key Statistics & Graphics*. Retrieved from Economic Research Service: https://www.ers.usda.gov/topics/food-nutrition-assistance/food-security-in-the-us/key-statistics-graphics#foodsecure

Very Well Mind. (2025, May 9). *What is Attachment Theory*. Retrieved from Very Well Mind: https://www.verywellmind.com/what-is-attachment-theory-2795337

Wolrich, D. J. (2021). *Food Isn't Medicine: Challenge Nutrib*llocks & Escape the Diet Trap*. London: Vermilion.

About the Author

Tiffany North (they/she) goes by their last name, North. As an RN, Integrative Nurse Coach, Certified Intuitive Eating Professional, and creator of the food and body attachment model, North helps people find freedom, balance, and satisfaction with food and body. Her passion is challenging the harmful systems of oppression and inequality, especially weight stigma and anti-fat bias. They have been sober since 1998 and feel that recovery has informed their work and all areas of their life. They live on the unceded lands of the Clackamas, Stl'pulmsh (Cowlitz), Cayuse, Umatilla, and Walla Walla Native tribes, and the Confederated Tribes of the Grand Ronde and Siletz Indians. North values the indigenous stewardship of these deeply nourishing lands. They love adventures of any size, whether it's going down a newly discovered alley or exploring glaciers in Iceland.

www.coachtiffanyrn.com
instagram.com/coachtiffanyrn
tiktok.com/@coachtiffanyrn
facebook.com/CoachTiffanyRN
youtube.com/@coachtiffanyrn